Even if you don't.

A love story

For Dr. Patrick Williams,

My friend and battle companion

"Even if God didn't do all these miracles, I knew I was going to be better off for believing. Even if He didn't, God would still have a plan. Even if He didn't, I was still going to believe, and ask, and expect miracles."

-Kailen Combs Taylor

Introduction

At End's Beginning

I was twenty-six the first time I died.

I stepped beyond the veil to stand at the edge of it all, looked out over the vast wasteland that awaited me, a barren reflection of my own madness. The world behind me once held warmth; in fleeting moments, I remember it. But I cannot go back. The veil is unyielding, impervious to my desperate pleas for re-entry.

It never made sense until I realized I'm not trapped inside the wasteland, but rather, the wasteland is trapped inside of me. I am victim and villain, both equally helpless.

So here I remain, in this empty ocean without shores, fighting the stale battles of a war I lost long ago. I often question if God made a mistake when He took the light from the world, leaving me to wander amid the shadows of cold and lifeless things, in the company of stone statues that never speak.

But then again, who am I?

I was twenty-six the first time I died. And I've died again every day since.

Part One

The Hand and the Heart

*"They slipped briskly into an intimacy from which
they never recovered."*

– F. Scott Fitzgerald, *This Side of Paradise*

We fell in the fall.

It was Sunday and I watched her climb the church steps, silhouetted by the neon glow of the stage. She had on a black jacket, her hands stuffed deep in the pockets as though she were grasping for something.

I would later discover her to be the coldest-natured person I had ever known. And the loveliest.

She sat two rows in front of me and I paid positively no attention to the sermon. I had my Bible open, pretending to take notes, but I don't remember a single thing about the service. All I know is that an hour later I was standing wide-eyed in the atrium, waiting for Erin Gatewood, one of my best friends, to introduce me.

Kailen was standing in the middle of a large circle of people, casually introducing herself to the few of us she hadn't met. We used to call our friend group the "Frankfort Crew," because except for me, that's where everyone grew up. Kailen already knew most of them through her friendship with Josh Hicks, who served as the social fulcrum for Frankfort and most of central Kentucky. He knew everybody, and if he didn't, he knew someone who did.

Finally, she looked at me. She wore a gray top beneath her leather jacket, skinny jeans on skinny legs, and short black boots. Her hair was pulled up and braided in the back. And her eyes were big and impossibly blue.

As fate would have it, I didn't realize until those magnificent eyes were staring at me that I had worn camouflage to church. Threadbare jeans, a camo fleece, and a camo hat, to be precise. I glanced over at Josh and very seriously considered punching him. Had he told me she was coming, I might have, you know, *not* worn hunting clothes.

"And this is Bryan," Erin said.

I was still thinking about hitting Josh but registered that someone had said my name. I turned and saw that

Even if you don't.

Kailen had stepped toward me. My heart lurched.

"Very nice to meet you, ma'am," I said, clenching my jaw to keep my voice from quivering.

We shook hands.

Erin continued on with introductions, making her way around the circle, but I kept staring at Kailen. She was introverted and you could tell the attention made her uncomfortable, but as the group migrated into the parking lot, I decided she was the most beautiful thing I had ever seen.

In reality, I had made that decision two months prior. But we'll get to that.

After more than an hour of loitering outside the church, a length of time that felt like mere seconds to me, everyone eventually climbed into their vehicles.

I made the incredibly stupid decision of going home to study while everyone else got together to have dinner and play ping pong. I found out the next day that several guys from the Frankfort Crew had hit on Kailen, and at least three had asked her out.

I wasn't mad. I had no right to be. Plus, I couldn't exactly blame them. I should have thrown my hat in the ring instead of studying chemistry like a blithering moron.

But lucky for me, they went o-for-three.

The handshake happened on November 1st, 2009 around 7:30 in the evening. But the story actually began on a balmy afternoon in September.

I lived in Grand Reserve at the time, an apartment complex in Lexington. They're advertised as luxury apartments, and while I'm not sure they were luxurious in the literal sense of the word, they were more than adequate for a college kid making seven bucks-an-hour at the local Wal-Mart.

The problem, as it were, wasn't the apartment. It was its animalistic inhabitants.

I lived with my best friend, Ben, who was dating Erin at the time, and he was pretty much the ideal roommate. He did things like clean his dishes, pick his clothes up out of the hallway, *not* leave shards of glass in the kitchen floor, that sort of stuff. I cannot say the same for our other two roommates.

I'm digressing, but suffice it to say I came back from Christmas break to find three feet of trash accumulation in the kitchen, what appeared to be a holocaust of ants in and around the fridge, and a mountainous stack of unread newspapers in the living room. The front door was also standing wide open, which had plunged the ambient room temperature into the thirties.

But in September it was balmy and I was studying in my recliner. Ben wasn't studying but Erin was, and they were sitting on his bed across the room from me. If you're wondering why we weren't in the living room, I would direct your attention back to the aforementioned newspapers and the incorrigible scent wafting from the

Even if you don't.

Ben was on Facebook and eventually Erin put her textbook away and joined him. I was still memorizing physics equations – because, clearly, I'm an overly-responsible nerd – when I overheard Erin mention one of her friends from Louisville.

"Who's Kailen?" I asked.

Erin was bright-eyed. "Oh, she's just the *sweetest*. Seriously, I think she's the best person I know. I could almost cry just thinking about her."

I was mostly unfazed and kept studying. Erin said that kind of stuff about everyone, even me. The *tap-tap* of their keys was annoying and I was about to put my headphones in when Erin said something else.

"And uh, she's single..."

I glanced up. "What's that, now?"

Erin laughed. "Just sayin'."

I tossed my physics in the floor and performed a very well-executed Facebook stalk. It was a thing of beauty, a veritable NSA-level breach of privacy. But it was superfluous. Her profile picture was enough.

She was flying through the air above a trampoline, a friend on either side of her. They were all attractive, and I remember thinking they might have been cousins they looked so similar, but Kailen immediately stood out. Though the other girls were smiling, Kailen was

13

laughing, her face contorted with uncontainable joy.

It was just a photograph, but I could tell, sitting there in my recliner, that Kailen Combs had an indomitable fervor for life.

Erin told me Kailen battled some health challenges, but you would never know it. She was always smiling, always talking about how good God is. And as I read through her posts it quickly became obvious. There were pictures from Mayo Clinic in Jacksonville, Florida, along with a blog entry or two. Not only was this woman gorgeous, and I mean straight-up *whoa* gorgeous, she loved Christ *and* she was a good writer.

Needless to say, my mind was already made up.

Fast forward back to November. My mundane life hasn't changed much – I'm still sitting in my recliner, studying who knows what – but there is one crucial difference: Kailen and I have now reached a serious milestone in our relationship, a momentous step forward in my courting efforts: we have become, *Facebook friends.*

You must know I'm Facebook's biggest critic. Mostly because I'm an old-fashioned curmudgeon who adores hardback books and prefers to be left alone. But I can tell you firsthand, it's a useful tool.

After she accepted my friend request – which prompted me to sprint out of my room, screaming and pumping my fists and admonishing my ape-like roommates to mind their own business – we started messaging one another. Just like the technological

Even if you don't.

moron I am, I was sending messages on her wall where everyone could see them. She informed me there was a way we could communicate with some level of privacy, and politely told me how.

We continued on like that for a few weeks, communicating once or twice a day, until finally I decided it was time to make a move. In very Don Draper fashion, my move was to tell the most elaborate lie of my young life.

And to my great surprise, it actually worked.

♥ ♥ ♥

It wasn't so much a lie as it was a deliberate geographical miscalculation. And it actually *didn't* work, at least not at first.

Kailen lived in La Grange, a small town just east of Louisville. I grew up in an even smaller town in western Kentucky, called Matanzas.

My miscalculation was that La Grange was "on my way" home. And seeing as I was going home to hunt the following weekend, it only made sense that I would stop by La Grange and take Kailen out for coffee.

She wasn't buying it. I guess she did something dramatic like consult a map.

But all wasn't lost. She told me she was coming back to Lexington the following week for a Kentucky basketball game. Her plan was to get into town early to see some friends, but if I played my cards right, maybe

15

just maybe those friends would make other plans. I guess I played the right cards because we made arrangements to meet up for coffee on campus, at Ovid's Café.

It was November 19th. Kentucky was playing Sam Houston State. I was in the basement of the library, what was called *The Hub* at the time, and had just tuned in to the KSR pre-game show when I was struck by another one of my brilliant ideas.

Hopping back on Facebook, which was quickly becoming my go-to dating assistant, I sent Kailen a message and told her I would come walk her from her car back to the library. It was getting dark, after all. Everyone knows campus isn't safe after dark. I gave her my phone number and told her to text me when she got to Lexington.

When she texted that she had arrived and would be okay walking by herself, I patted myself on the back. I had successfully gotten her phone number without even having to ask. *What a clever tactician I was.* Much later, Kailen admitted she had immediately recognized the ploy and merely humored me by replying.

That was something that would go on to happen many times in our relationship – Kailen humoring my delusions of grandeur.

I shouldered my backpack and hurried upstairs to Ovid's, where I grabbed us a table by the window. I got a little nervous while I waited, but I wasn't wearing camo this time and felt good about that. I pretended to flip through a newspaper until I saw her walk by the

My memory isn't fully photographic, but when it comes to certain subjects it's quite close. One of those subjects is Kailen. If you pick a day, a time, a place, or an event, I can tell you what she was wearing, how her hair was fixed, what her perfume smelled like, or just about any other detail you'd like to know.

On that night at Ovid's, she was wearing jeans, a dark fleece over a blue blouse, and a blue-checkered infinity scarf. Her long brown hair was down, but she had curled it near the ends, causing it to cascade over her shoulders in waves. She had worn it up during our first meeting at church and I liked it. But I *loved* it down.

I would typically tell you there's a difference between cute and sexy, but Kailen found a way to meld them into one mesmerizing draught.

Her cheeks were rosy from the cool air, and when she smiled, they got rosier. It was months later before she admitted the red cheeks weren't from the cold, but rather from surprise when I stood up. She hadn't realized how tall I was. And while I don't consider myself particularly handsome, I'm sure glad she thought so.

I met her by the door and we shook hands again, albeit a little less business-like this time around.

"How was the drive?" I asked, grinning like a child.

She flashed her dimples. "It was good. I beat the

17

game traffic."

Despite communicating daily for almost three weeks, that was the first time I heard her voice. It was deeper than I imagined and I was incredibly attracted to the sound. She spoke with confidence and eloquence, revealing a maturity far beyond her nineteen years.

We fell fluidly into conversation as we waited in line at Starbucks. At the risk of being cliché, it was like we had known each other for years. She told me about her brother, who played football at Oldham County, and her sister, who loved to play piano. Her dad was a businessman and her mom was an administrative assistant at church. By the time we ordered, I felt like I knew them, too.

Kailen ordered a white chocolate mocha, which is what I wanted, but I needed to make an impression. So I opted for a man's drink, a plain black coffee, and choked it down honorably.

We sat and talked about movies, books, faith, and Kentucky basketball. She was extremely excited about Coach John Calipari and what he had done for the program since his arrival.

I liked her before, but now I was smitten.

At one point, she spilled her coffee on her fleece and turned rosy again. She laughed aloud when I offered to spill mine, too. We laughed at that, then something else, then forgot why we were laughing. It was the most wonderful forty-five minutes of my life.

Even if you don't.

I thought nothing of the fact that she had gotten up to go to the bathroom five or six times, nor did I have any idea that she hadn't eaten anything that day. I was a clueless kid, blissfully unaware, unburdened by the weight of the world.

She might have acted unburdened, but she was anything but clueless. She hadn't been a kid in a long, long time.

We finished our coffee and I walked her to Blazer Hall, where she was meeting a friend for dinner before the game. She shivered in the cold and I held her hand. Her skin was soft, her fingers long. I squeezed, interlocking them with my own.

She tried to say bye outside Blazer, but I would have none of it. I told her I wanted to meet her friend. Again, *impressions.*

I introduced myself to Kathryn, the girl that would become Kailen's roommate when she re-enrolled at UK in the spring, and finally left them alone so they could eat. But as I stepped into the night air, I looked back in through the window.

She was still watching me, and she was smiling.

Five days later, on November 24th, I pulled my Chevy pick-up into the driveway outside the Combs' residence. I tried to breathe but couldn't seem to figure it out; I would have given my left arm for a Valium.

19

Kailen and I had texted prolifically following our coffee date and she eventually invited me to her house. When I told her I would just stop by *on my way* home for Thanksgiving, she probably laughed and said something like, "You're such an idiot."

And she was right. If being an idiot meant I got to be with her, then an idiot is what I intended to be.

I forced my shaky legs to move and climbed out of the truck. When I did, the front door opened and Kailen stepped onto the porch. Their family dog, a boxer named Zoe, met me in the yard, and though I knelt down to pet her, I couldn't take my eyes off the porch. Somehow, she looked even more beautiful. She had on the same jeans from Ovid's, along with a long-sleeve navy blue shirt. Her hair was straight and pulled into a ponytail.

"Hey there," she said.

I'd never wanted to hug someone so badly in all my life, but I didn't. This wasn't just some girl. And this wasn't just some moment. She smiled and led the way inside.

Kentucky played Cleveland State that night, at the Cancun Challenge. They played on a shoddy ballroom floor and chandeliers dangled into the camera view from somewhere high above. Kentucky won handily, but for the first time in my life, I couldn't have cared less.

I met her mom, Kim, and her dad, Jeff, and later I met her siblings, Jarrod and Kristen. When Jarrod took me downstairs to show me his prized deer head mounted on the wall, I knew I was in.

We all sat on two oversized leather couches and talked for hours. Long after the game ended, the conversation seemed to continue on effortlessly, just as it had at Ovid's. Kim still jabs me about how closely I sat to Kailen, our thighs pressed against one another. I wanted to blame the couch, but it was so huge that wouldn't work. In the end, I was honest and confessed that no amount of closeness could have ever been close enough.

It was an amazing night, and by two in the morning, I was thinking it couldn't have gone any better. Which is exactly the moment I messed up.

As I was getting ready to leave, I shook Jarrod and Jeff's hands, but Kim came in for the hug. And that was perfectly fine with me. In fact, I loved it. It served to further convince me that the night had been a success.

But when I pulled out of the embrace, my nerves finally got the best of me.

"What was your name again?" I asked.

I knew it immediately. I looked over at Kailen, who was wide-eyed and turning redder by the second. And this time it had nothing to do with my dashing good looks. I could have crawled in a hole; I had been so very close to making it out alive.

I don't remember exactly what happened after that, but when I regained consciousness, Kailen had walked me out onto the porch. She was smiling, which I took as a good sign.

"Thanks for coming," she told me, her smooth voice melting away my anxiety. "I really enjoyed it. I know it's a little out of the way." She winked.

That overwhelming hug-urge returned, but again I resisted. I shook her hand, much like I had that night at church, but then I lifted it and lightly kissed the tips of her fingers. She blushed and I'm sure I did, too. But I think we both enjoyed it – I *know* I did.

I'm pretty sure I didn't turn the radio on the entire way home. I actually was headed back to Matanzas for Thanksgiving, and I spent the two-hour drive remembering the taste of her fingers, the lightning sensation of her thigh grazing against mine.

Meanwhile, back in La Grange, Kim and Jeff were lying in bed determining my fate. They have since told me the story:

"I don't know about him," Kim said. "He scares me."

"Why's that?" Jeff asked, slipping ever-closer toward sleep.

"She likes him. Maybe *too* much. Plus, he forgot my name."

Jeff laughed.

"What?"

Even if you don't.

More laughter.

"What?!" Kim wanted to know.

Then Jeff rolled over. "Kim, sweetie, I think you just met your future son-in-law."

Jeffery, I know I've told you a thousand times before, but *thank you*, my friend. I'll forever be in your debt.

♥ ♥ ♥

I was waiting on the sidewalk, my breath coming out in little white coils, when Kailen came bee-boppin' out of the Funkhouser Building.

That's a minor but important fact – Kailen didn't walk, she bee-bopped. It was a sort of skip-hop without the skip or the hop; if you watched her legs you would have just thought she was walking normally, but somehow her shoulders and hips seemed to bounce as she gained momentum.

I always postulated it had something to do with that whole *indomitable fervor for life* thing.

It was the first week of December and Kailen had come back to UK to re-enroll for the spring semester. We were now talking on the phone at least once-a-day and texting as often as our fingers would allow. We hadn't arrived at the hugging phase yet, but we were firmly entrenched in the hand-holding phase and I was a man content with his lot in life.

23

I did, however, sneak a pseudo-side-hug as she walked up to me on the sidewalk.

Same jeans, cream fleece, brown scarf, tan Sperry's. She had also done that wavy thing with her hair again, which I adored, but it was a little curlier this time, so it merely graced the tops of her shoulders instead of cascading over them.

"Where we headed?" I asked, secretly hoping it was somewhere miles away so I could keep holding her hand.

"Gotta get some books," she told me. "Then you can buy me lunch."

Again, the hug-urge. "Sounds like a deal," I said.

We spent an hour at University Book Store, perusing online syllabi and assembling Kailen's armamentarium of textbooks, planners, pens, post-it notes, folders, binders, tab dividers, and, did I already say post-it notes? This woman was organized. She and I shared a little OCD-predilection, but her post-it note fetish was all her own.

While we shopped, and the stack of items piled in my arms steadily grew, she told me a little about why she had withdrawn from school in the first place. She had completed her freshman year at UK before health concerns had forced her to sit a semester out. She still didn't tell me exactly what it was, but she told me about her trip to Jacksonville, where she saw a specialist at Mayo Clinic. I remembered seeing a picture on her Facebook from the trip, one where she was sitting on a

Even if you don't.

wooden swing, her bare feet in the grass, Spanish moss shrouding her on all sides.

She had looked so healthy, I thought to myself. She *looks* so healthy.

"*Ugg!*" she said, rolling her eyes. "This song is *so* cheeseball."

I was confused for a moment, then realized the bookstore was playing Christmas music. *Wonderful Christmastime*, by Paul McCartney had just come on.

"What does cheeseball mean?" I asked.

She laughed, more *at* me than with me, and never answered. To be fair, I still don't know with certainty. I assume it means cheesy or gimmicky, but Kailen-language can be tricky even for a veteran, much less a beginner.

I don't recall precisely what we were talking about when we left the bookstore, but it must have been important because Kailen ordered a pinky promise. Now this is yet another nuance of Kailen-language. Like most people, I thought a pinky promise was when you looped your pinkies together and made some kind of privacy pact or assurance of discretion. But Kailen wasn't like most people, and she wasted no time telling me I was wrong.

A proper pinky promise, she explained, was performed by looping your pinkies together, making the promise, then kissing the back of your hand to formally solidify the arrangement.

I did not, in any way, understand what she meant. But it seemed simple enough. So, when we looped pinkies, I moved confidently in for the kiss.

Her eyes grew to the size of grapefruits. *"What are you doing?!"*

"Um, well, I thought we were making a pinky promise."

"You did it wrong," she scoffed, her eyes shrinking back down somewhere in the vicinity of tangerines. "You're supposed to kiss *your* hand, not mine."

My mistake, as it were, was not kissing her hand. She had already proven that, at worst, she didn't mind when I kissed her hand, or at best, she actually enjoyed it a little. The hand-kissing wasn't the problem. The problem was in the logistics. Because when I kissed the back of her hand, she was *also* kissing the back of her hand per proper pinky promise protocol. That meant our lips were approximately 1.25 centimeters apart, which equates to about half-an-inch.

I've never officially confessed to purposefully breaching pinky promise protocol, but when you consider the fact that I was a twenty-year-old male saturated with hug-urge, I'll let you draw your own conclusion.

The scandal eventually dissipated and we bee-bopped our way to Firehouse Subs, a few blocks from the bookstore. We sat in the corner by the window, at a little red table with misshapen legs, and talked for almost three hours. People came and went and sunlight

Even if you don't.

faded.

It was dark by the time we walked back to R-Lot, where her car was parked. I held her hand the whole way, felt her long fingers curl into mine. We were discussing when we might get to see one another again, but my mind was elsewhere. It was back at Firehouse. Because this time I'd paid more attention – eleven bathroom visits in three hours.

I have no idea how she knew what I was thinking, but she did.

On cue, she squeezed my hand. "There's something I need to tell you."

I squeezed back but didn't say anything. I looked into her eyes, saw the weight gathered there.

"I was made to do hard things," she explained. "God told me when I was a little girl. He said my life wouldn't be easy, that it would be painful, and He's been right so far." She paused and glanced away before adding, "So if you don't want to do hard things, I'm not sure we'll work out."

We all have moments in our life that define us. The scene from *Good Will Hunting* where Robin Williams hugs Matt Damon comes to mind. Moments that restructure our souls, moments that reroute our path and establish our destiny. We often have a choice in these moments, to either accept the new route or stay the course, to embrace destiny or decline it.

We were back at the car and she was staring over at

27

me, her piercing blue eyes searching my soul. I've always been a touch cynical when it comes to God speaking audibly, but I knew she was telling the truth. She *was* made to do hard things. God had chosen her, and for some reason far beyond my comprehension, He had chosen me as well.

"I wanna do hard things," I told her. "If it means I get to do them with you."

She didn't believe me at first. Other guys had undoubtedly told her the same thing, and the sting of broken promises was written all over her face.

But I wasn't other guys.

Finally, she smiled and said, "Ok, then."

Then she turned up the radio and started dancing.

I sipped diabetically-sweet tea and breathed a sigh of relief. It was December 16th and final exams were over.

Ben and I were sitting in a booth at Raising Canes, a campus fried-chicken favorite. All told, the tea, the fries, the chicken, and the heroin-like sauce were a great way to spend an afternoon seriously harming your health.

"I'm gonna do it," I told him. "I'm gonna go for it."

"That's great," he mumbled, gnawing on a tender.

Even if you don't.

"I already texted her parents, so I think we're good there."

He was still chewing. "Yep, very well done."

Ben was actually pretty excited for me, I think, even though he did a poor job of showing it. I would have been frustrated with him if it weren't for that sauce – it was transcendently delicious, which made interpersonal communication difficult.

I was a man with a plan. After I finished my post-exam celebratory meal, I texted Kailen and told her I had just eaten lunch with Ben – a truth – and now I was headed back home to write a paper that was due the next day – a complete fabrication. Kailen was nothing if not gullible and she took the bait hook, line, and sinker.

What I actually did was throw my bags in my truck and hop on Interstate 64. I had only seen Kailen once since I told her I wanted to do hard things, and progress seemed to be stagnating. We were texting and talking, but I had my eyes firmly fixed on hug phase.

I'm talking dangerous accumulations of hug-urge at this point, folks.

By the time I made it to La Grange, I was trembling with excitement. There are few things in life I love more than a surprise. Little did I know Kailen wasn't a big fan of unannounced arrivals, but I taught her to love them. She didn't have much choice in the matter.

I parked down the street and crept through several yards until I was behind her house. Moving in a very thief-like crouch – I'm glad no one called the cops – I snuck around front and carefully placed a book on her front porch, along with a white rose. The book was called *Captivating*, by John and Stasi Eldredge. It was the feminine counterpart to *Wild at Heart*, a book Kailen and I had spent hours discussing. Also, it very much described how I felt about her. To say I was captivated would have been an understatement.

I scurried back behind the house and called her.

"How's the paper coming?" she asked.

I could hear her voice through the wall. My adrenaline surged.

"Very well," I lied. "Making good progress. By the way, you may want to go check your front porch."

There was a pause. "What?"

"I may or may not have sent you something."

I had sent flowers to her house a few weeks prior, so I hoped she thought I was getting unimaginative.

Moments later, the front door opened and there were footsteps on the porch. When I heard her squeal, I could have just about cried.

Then I made my move.

"What do you think?" I asked, still talking through the phone.

Even if you don't.

"I love it!" she yelled. "Thank you so mu—"

I came around the side of the house and she screamed, then squealed again. When I climbed onto the porch, I could see little tears forming in her eyes. I've never felt warmth like that. All I know to say is the moment was magic, pure fluid magic.

"Good afternoon," I told her. "You look beautiful."

She swayed a little, then swallowed hard as several little tears became a big tear and slipped down her cheek. She smiled.

"I look a mess," she said.

She had on pajama pants, a navy pullover, and a red apron covered in flour. Her hair was mostly in a ponytail, but there were strands that had edged out and fallen onto her face. On her feet were little brown house shoes, Ugg brand. I did a good job of hiding the fact that her beauty, once again, made me feel mildly asthmatic.

I caught my breath and said, "I've never seen such an elegant mess in all my life."

Another tear fell, and though she didn't say anything, her eyes told the story. I didn't hesitate and I didn't ask permission. Right there on her front porch, for the whole world to see, I wrapped my arms around her and pulled her tight against me. When I felt her arms around me as well, the heavens rejoiced.

Hallelujah! Holy hug-phase!

31

♥ ♥ ♥

I spent the next two days at the Combs' house. You may find that a little quick or presumptive, but I swear it was like we were already family. I mean, when you consider the fact that I had *hugged* their daughter, it kind of makes sense.

We spent the rest of Wednesday afternoon and evening baking cookies and making Christmas candy. Things got a little wild and I ended up wearing the apron, but I make a mean buckeye and a good time was had by all.

That night, a ping pong tournament was held in the basement. The first round was a breeze, the second round posed no challenge, but the finals showdown was inarguably epic.

Picture the scene: Kailen, Kim, and Kristen are in the crowd, Jeff's officiating, and Jarrod and I are squared off in a battle for the ages. It came down to game-point, then another, then another, and another. The final tally was 30-28. I won't tell you who won, but it wasn't Jarrod.

We watched a movie upstairs in the living room – *The Matrix*, I believe it was – until everyone started falling asleep. Kailen and I were the last survivors and it was nearly dawn before we gave up the fight. She went upstairs to her room and I slept on one of the couches. Though they were huge, they weren't terribly long and I woke up from my two-hour nap with at least four misplaced vertebrae.

Even if you don't.

Breakfast, I soon discovered, was a Jeff Combs specialty. Blueberry pancakes, sausage, bacon, eggs, toast, skillet potatoes, gravy, and French-pressed coffee. It was excessive, but Jarrod and I put on an eating clinic and leftovers were minimal. The rest of the day was spent making more cookies, lounging around watching Christmas movies, and brief stints of ping pong in an attempt to repair Jarrod's wounded manhood.

After dinner and movies on Thursday night, Kailen and I were once again left alone in the living room. If Jeff and Kim were wondering why on earth I was still at their house, they were polite and didn't show it. Either that, or the answer was obvious.

As the clock crept toward midnight, I told Kailen she might need to go look inside *Captivating*. She gave me a curious look, then hurried up to her room.

I sat on the couch while she read the letter I had hidden inside the book. The TV was off but the Christmas tree was on, and I waited anxiously in its ivory glow.

Several minutes later, I heard her coming down the steps. I sat up straight and tried to act confident as she bee-bopped over to me, an unreadable expression on her face.

I stood up and smiled down at her. "What'd you think?"

"I think there's something you need to ask me," she said, raising her eyebrows.

I nodded and snapped a mental image. I can see it, her perfect face silhouetted by the tree light, the scent of vanilla and cinnamon wafting from a candle somewhere behind us.

"Will you be my girlfriend?" I asked.

It came out like an exhale, more instinct than actual cognition.

Only then did she smile. "Yes, Bryan Taylor, I will."

Suddenly the hug-urge was something more. I placed my hands gently on her shoulders and stepped closer.

"May I kiss you, ma'am?"

Her grin was mischievous, but her nod was certain.

Our lips met for the first time beside her parents' Christmas tree at 12:04 AM on December 18th, 2009. They met again at 12:05, and that time, I didn't ask.

♥ ♥ ♥

We turned the piano into a sniper's nest. There were ferns stacked on every side and Ben was pressed flat on his stomach underneath it, a camera peeking out between the leaves. He gave me the thumbs-up and I killed the lights.

245 days had passed, right at eight months, since the gleeful frolicking beneath the Christmas tree. And Kailen and I had wasted no time figuring out how to do

life together.

I spent a few days in La Grange for Christmas, then she made the westward trek to Matanzas to meet my family. She found the Taylor clan was nice and surprisingly sophisticated for forest people that burn their own trash, and my mom and sisters fell in love with her even quicker than I did.

That first Christmas, Kailen and I bought one another almost identical gifts – two books and a journal. One of the books she got me was titled, *Yankees Suck,* and as a lifelong Red Sox fan, I think that was the moment I knew I was going to marry her.

In January, Kim and Jeff surprised me by letting Kailen accompany me to Florida for a friend's wedding. We rode down with Ben and Erin and a prolific friendship was born. Ben and I had been friends most of our lives – he, too, was from Matanzas – but we could barely get a word in edgewise. Kailen and Erin simply would not shut up. It was a beautiful thing, the foundational tenets of a story yet to be told, so I just held her hand and enjoyed the ride.

In mid-February, I wrecked Jeff's Range Rover. Yeah, I'm cringing too.

I could waste thousands of words blaming the incident on the grossly irresponsible drainage practices of the Blazer Hall kitchen, but I actually want this book to get published. So, suffice it to say I slid Jeff's $80,000 vehicle down a hill, across an intersection, and implanted it into the back-end of a $2,500 Chevy. Had there been a bridge within walking distance, I would have been in headfirst descent. But seeing as my feet were still on the ground, and my girlfriend's dad's Range Rover was physically attached to a truck driven by a man named Homer, I began considering what body fluids I could sell to pay for the damage. In the end, Jeff forgave me. But Kailen's uncles started calling me "Crash" and some of them still do.

Two months later, on a trip to Matanzas, two significant events transpired. One, Kailen met my papaw. Papaw had long-been my hero, but he had been my best friend for longer than that. When Kailen shook his hand in Mamaw and Papaw's basement, I knew it was the melding of worlds, the intersection of past and future. I snapped another mental image.

The second event happened the next night, when I was tucking Kailen into bed. She was sleeping in my room while I slept on an air mattress in the living room. We didn't have any fancy oversize couches in Matanzas, but the air mattress was actually a touch superior when it came to my spinal health.

But back to the point – I was tucking her in, and as you might imagine, hug-urge is a relic at this juncture. I now have much bigger problems. But as I knelt down and prayed, I wasn't thinking about urges or problems; I was busy making the most significant realization of my life.

"I think I love you," I told her, after the prayer.

She smiled resiliently. "I think you do, too."

That spring we watched, heartbroken, as Kentucky

lost to West Virginia in the Elite Eight, and then a few weeks later we cheered Phil Mickelson to a win at Augusta. Those became our two favorite sporting events – March Madness and the Masters – and we watched them together every year, without fail.

I was gone to Birmingham for seven weeks during the summer, working at an abandoned gas station my uncle had transformed into a fireworks store, and when I got back I met a new version of Kailen – I met *tan* Kailen.

If the problems I was having in March were grenades, they were full-scale nuclear warheads by June.

It was striking, though, the thought that if she could get that much more beautiful in seven weeks, what could she do with seven *years*? Or seventy?

At the end of July, we laid in the back of Papaw's truck and gazed up at a blanket of stars unfurling over Matanzas. We were parked high on a hill and there were no clouds; we had an unimpeded view of the heavens. *Clarity.* That's what it was, both in the summer sky and in my heart.

For that was the night I made my decision.

August 20th, 2010 – Ben's in the sniper's nest and I'm sitting on a stool a few yards away from him. We're both in the sanctuary of New Life, the church where Kailen grew up.

A few weeks prior, sometime before our night of

star-gazing, Kailen had told me about her "husband spot." When they were constructing the building, the pastor had encouraged church members to write scriptures and prayer requests on studs, support beams, concrete walls, or anything else they could find. A church, he said, should be rooted in prayer.

As the mother of three young children, Kim had a smart idea – she instructed each of her kids to use this opportunity to pray for their future spouse. Using sharpies, they each found a spot and made their mark.

Kristen's husband.
Kailen's husband.
Jarrod's wife.

My stool was parked twelve feet to the left of the stage. It wasn't actually twelve feet, it was twelve of *Kailen's* feet; ever-meticulous, even as a kid, she had stepped it off toe-to-heel, that way she would always know precisely where to pray for her husband.

When the sanctuary doors opened, the lights came on and the music started. *History in the Making,* by Darius Rucker, was our song and it rang into the rafters.

I watched Kailen's shock slowly transform to realization as Erin and Kim led her into the room. The song, the lighting, *where* I was sitting – it all started falling into place.

Scattered down the aisle were notes I had written her, each accompanied by some significant artifact of our relationship. One item was my coffee cup from our first night at Ovid's, another was a napkin from our lunch at Firehouse, and there was also a ticket stub from the night we watched Kentucky beat Drexel for their 2000th win.

There were several others, and it took her the better part of five minutes to finally get to me. When she did, I stood up and held her hands, surreptitiously glancing over her shoulder at the sniper's nest. Ben had the camera right on us.

So as the chorus of our song echoed throughout the sanctuary, a thin layer of drywall the only thing separating me from Kailen's husband spot, I dropped onto one knee and asked her to marry me.

I said something like, "Kailen Olivia Mae, will you be my wife?"

Her eyes glistened, her mouth gaped, and she said the only thing she knew to say:

She squealed.

Part Two

The Bend in the Road

"I will not let my joy be stolen by troubles this world calls undeserved."

– Kailen

I've never been a partyer. Throughout high school and college, I was more of the class-practice-study-sleep type. But when I decided to marry into the Combs family, I very quickly earned a crash course in how to do it right.

After Kailen agreed to marry me, we went out to dinner at the Cheesecake Factory, then came home to a houseful of people. Kailen's family was huge and none considered themselves extended – everyone was immediate. I didn't do an exact head count, but there had to be at least thirty aunts, uncles, cousins, second-cousins, and grandparents, all gathered together to celebrate. Jeff and Ben got the video set up in the living room and everyone watched the proposal.

There were *oohs*, *ahhs*, and tears, and afterward, handshakes and hugs. I'd never felt so loved by so many, and I remember being humbled that such an amazing and Godly family would choose to accept me into its ranks.

That night, I had my first cigar. Ben, Jarrod, and I sat on the back porch and talked like old men, awkwardly puffing on the celebratory stogies Jeff had bought for us. Jarrod was the seasoned professional of the group – he had smoked no less than *four* cigars in his day – and he kindly offered to show us the ropes.

It was a warm evening and I remember sweat dripping down my face as I watched the women laughing in the living room behind us. They were gathered on the couches and their conversation looked to be riveting. Jeff had joined the men on the porch, but when he stepped back inside to refill his drink, the three of us took the opportunity to discuss sex.

Considering we were all virgins, there wasn't much to talk about. So when the silence became awkward, which didn't take long, we made our way out into the yard and looked up at the stars, still puffing gingerly on the cigars.

41

Ben and Erin decided to stay the weekend and we spent Saturday making preliminary wedding plans. We went to bed really late, sometime around three, and my phone woke me before six on Sunday morning.

It was mom. Though I could hear her voice, it took a while to register what she was telling me. I was groggy and half-asleep, but that wasn't the reason for the delayed understanding. My heart just didn't want to believe what my brain was processing.

My papaw had died. He had passed peacefully, she told me, in his sleep. He had died at home, in his own bed, and that's how he would have wanted it. It was true, of course, but that small consolation didn't stop my heart from breaking.

I went for a drive shortly after sunrise. It was a beautiful morning, the 22nd day of August, and I watched fog linger above the fields before the summer heat burned it off. I was driving too fast and didn't know where I was going, so I didn't make any turns. I just drove straight on the same road for almost an hour, sobbing like a child.

It was my first experience with death and I had no idea what to do with the void; the thought of my hero no longer being in the world was not only crushing, but confusing. I couldn't make sense of it.

So I cried until the tears stopped, then turned around and drove back.

Ben met me on the sidewalk; Mom had told him the news. I wept on his shoulder until Kailen came out, then I wept on hers. Eventually we made it inside and sat at the kitchen table. Jeff had made breakfast and coffee and there was a warm plate waiting for me. I was too nauseous to eat, but I sipped my coffee while everyone else had breakfast.

That morning, less than forty-eight hours into my and Kailen's engagement, I learned three critical lessons: one about God, one about Kailen, and one about myself.

First, God never wastes pain. It's a sort of divine curriculum. It always serves a purpose, whether we recognize it at the time or not. And we often don't.

Second, Kailen was a one-woman support system. Her touch and her words not only numbed the pain, they helped heal it.

And third, there was a strength inside me I didn't know existed until that hot August morning.

Unbeknownst to me, God was using my pain to nurture and grow a seed He had planted long ago. I was thankful for the strength, but I was still just a kid. I had no way of knowing how badly I was going to need it.

I didn't realize until our engagement how little I knew about Kailen's health.

Though she had told me some about ulcerative colitis, the condition that caused her to go to the bathroom upwards of twenty times each day, my understanding was superficial at best. Outside of carrying her across campus and taking her to the ER when she was so anemic she could barely breathe, I had minimal experience with her illness. All I'd seen was the iceberg above the surface; what lay beneath was unfathomable.

Her health battle started on the first night of her life. She was born at 2:40 in the afternoon on February 24th, 1990. By midnight, her left lung had collapsed.

Though the lung eventually re-inflated, Kailen spent the first two weeks of her life in Kosair Children's Hospital. I recently sat down with Kim and Jeff and they told me one of the hardest things about the experience was not getting to enjoy her like normal parents would. The moments were precious, but they were fleeting, and by the time Kim and Jeff arrived at Kosair, their little girl had a tube inserted in her chest and a respirator attached to her face.

Kailen's survival was uncertain, but the doctor told them there were three things working in her favor: "One, she's a girl and girls are fighters. Two, she has a good birth weight. And three, she has a helluva temper."

When they injected Kailen with anesthetic prior to placing the chest tube, she had held her breath in protest. When she refused to start breathing again, they had no choice but to put her on a respirator. In over two decades of caring for newborns, the doctor said he had never seen anything like it.

She was feisty and stubborn, right from the

Even if you don't.

beginning.

Two weeks later, Kim and Jeff finally took Kailen home, and in typical Combs family fashion, they had a huge celebration.

Kailen was hospitalized again when she was two years old, with a left lung pneumonia, then had repeat pneumonias in the same lung each of the next three years. The doctors said it was a byproduct of the pneumothorax she had at birth and was likely something she would deal with throughout her youth and again in her elderly years.

But from the age of five through her second year of middle school, Kailen had a normal life. There were no major health crises, at least none Kim and Jeff knew about. She loved spending time outside, climbing trees, and writing in her journal. It quickly became apparent that Kailen had a gift when it came to writing. Her journal entries possessed the voice and creativity of someone who had spent years mastering the craft.

Here's a story she wrote about one of her tree-climbing adventures. It's entitled, *Maple*. She wrote it when she was nine years old:

"I'll beat you up to the top!" I yelled to my brother, Jarrod.

We were in a frantic hurry to our maple tree. I clung on the lowest branch. The bark felt smooth yet rough under my sweaty hands. Her leaves looked a little clear green with the sun shining on them. The higher I got the closer the branches were.

45

Bryan C. Taylor

When I got as high as I could get, I inched along a thick sturdy branch. This was my favorite spot, because here I imagined I was anything. The sun shined the most here, so it looked like everything I wanted to be. It was my perfect place.

Kailen lived her life with a perpetual sense of wonder, as evidenced by her poem, *Winter Night.* Again, she was nine:

My feet crunch upon the crisp snow.

I'm busy making clouds with my breath.

All I hear is myself.

My cheeks are rosy.

Everything is still except the gently-swaying snowflakes.

I lie down and think winter nights are beautiful.

For Kailen, every day possessed its own mystery. There was magic in the dust. She wrote this in her journal that same year:

All day long I think lots of thoughts,
Of very strange things
Like how waves are caught,
Or where the moon hides
While waiting its turn?
Why do we even have to learn?
Why is there spring,
Summer, winter, and fall?

Even if you don't.

Why does the breeze blow at all?
What does clay ponder while it hardens?
Do all the stars come from
Magic star gardens?
What would a plump purple plum
Say while getting picked?
What would a ball yell
While getting kicked?
What magic hides beneath the dust?
Who are the friends I can trust?
All day long I think lots of thoughts,
Of very strange things
Like how waves are caught

Her literary prowess wasn't limited to her journals, however. In 8th grade, she earned the highest score on the on-demand writing portion of the state standardized test in the history of Oldham County Middle School. Later that year, she got a congratulatory letter from President George W. Bush.

But neither Kailen's gifts nor her sense of wonder could shield her from the hard things she was meant to do.

When she was twelve she came down with a nasty stomach virus. It came with the usual symptoms – fever, diarrhea, and vomiting. The illness lasted longer than expected, but after a week or so, the vomiting cleared up and Kailen returned to her normal quirky self. She was a straight-A student and the president of her class.

It wasn't until almost a year later that Kim found diarrhea splattered on the wall behind the toilet in the kids' bathroom. When she asked Kailen about it, Kailen finally admitted that the diarrhea had never gone away. Kim took her to see her primary care physician, who ordered a test for clostridium difficile, also known as *C. Diff*, and put Kailen on antibiotic therapy. The *C. Diff* test came back negative, Kailen finished the antibiotics, and that was that.

But still Kailen kept her secret. The diarrhea hadn't gone away. In fact, it had gotten worse.

Years later, Kim found a journal entry Kailen had written in fifth grade. She was ten at the time. In it, she talked about her stomach troubles, and wrote that she had been using the bathroom more than fifteen times every night. It seemed the stomach virus had merely revealed a problem that had already been present for years.

As Kailen entered high school, Kim started occasionally finding underwear in the trash can. Kailen always downplayed the problem, but when Kim took her back to primary care, he referred them on to a pediatric gastroenterologist.

Kailen was fifteen when she had her first colonoscopy, an esophagogastroduodenal colonoscopy to be precise. Commonly called an EGD, this is a procedure that visualizes the entire gastrointestinal tract. The results were not good.

The pediatric gastro met Kim and Jeff in the waiting room and told them the news:

"She has esophagitis, gastritis, hiatal hernia, and

inflammation all throughout her colon. Basically, she's inflamed from her esophagus to her rectum. She has inflammatory bowel disease, either Crohn's or ulcerative colitis, doesn't really matter which. They're both treated the same way. It's chronic and she'll deal with it for the rest of her life."

The results were staccato and the doctor's voice was bereft of all emotion. As any parent would be, Kim and Jeff were stunned and heartbroken. Jeff also remembers wanting to smack the doctor for her callousness.

Kailen was initiated on an enormous cocktail of medication. She was taking as many as twelve pills a day, mostly mesalamines, a drug class that targets gastrointestinal inflammation. The pediatric gastro had also mentioned an immunosuppressant medication called Remicade. But after doing some research, Kim and Jeff firmly said no.

The mesalamines were only modestly effective and Kailen continued going to the bathroom dozens of times a day. And shortly after she turned sixteen, things actually got worse.

It was pneumonia again. Only this time it had formed a secondary abscess in the lower lobe of her left lung. When an x-ray revealed the abscess was the size of an orange, the primary care doctor again referred Kailen, this time to a pulmonologist. He prayed over her before she left his office; a lung abscess can be a fatal diagnosis, even for a young person. But when Kailen arrived at the hospital, the pulmonologist did a repeat x-ray and was baffled by the results.

The abscess had vanished.

It was the first of several miracles that would take place during Kailen's teenage years. There was no medical explanation, but there was also no denying the abscess had been there and now it was gone. The pulmonologist sent Kailen home and antibiotics healed the pneumonia within a few days.

Another brief period of normality followed as Kailen progressed through high school. She went on dates, thrived in her youth group at church, and continued excelling in her studies. She was a 4.0 student and a staple in the top tier of class leadership. In every aspect, Kailen Combs was exemplary. She humbly succeeded in every endeavor she embarked upon, all while spending five to six hours a day in the bathroom. Her joy and ambition were immutable.

But the normality came to an abrupt halt on February 28th, 2008, four days after Kailen turned eighteen. It was a Thursday. She had skipped church the night before to watch Kentucky play Ole Miss and had done a workout after the game. Little did she know, while she was busy doing squat thrusts, she came literal inches from death.

Kim was at work when she received a call from the athletic trainer at Kailen's high school. It was mid-morning, sometime before lunch. The AT's voice was wrought with trepidation. Kailen was in his office and her left leg was purple and very swollen. She had on skinny jeans, but the left pant leg was so tight he had considered cutting it to make room. After conferring with the physician that managed the sports teams, he was fairly certain Kailen had a blood clot.

Something you should know is that, while Kim Combs isn't a medical professional, her medical acumen far exceeds the average layperson. Though she never pursued any medical education – she studied music at University of the Cumberlands and is a fine pianist to this day – all her training was earned in the field. Kailen's life was basically one long medical residency for Kim, so by February 2008, responding to a medical emergency was second-nature.

She and Jeff had Kailen at the Baptist East ER within the hour. The emergency room physician performed a series of tests, including a Doppler of Kailen's leg. Though it had all the tell-tale signs of a clot – swollen, discolored, change in temperature – the ER doc came back and told them no clot was present. The symptoms were from something else.

When Kim asked what else it could be, his response was the height of negligence:

"You got me."

That wasn't a good enough answer, and while the nurse came into the room with discharge papers, Kim left to call Kailen's primary care doctor, a close family friend and a member of their church. When Kim told the ER physician who she was talking to, he agreed to confer with the primary care in an attempt to reach a more definitive conclusion.

A consensus was reached and an abdominal/pelvic CT scan was performed. When the doctor came back into the room this time, the news was very different.

The CT scan had revealed a massive clot in Kailen's pelvis. It was located in the left common iliac vein and had sprung other clots. Her lungs were full of pulmonary emboli, which are blood clots that have traveled throughout the circulatory system and deposited in the lungs. Just one pulmonary embolus can be fatal; Kailen had several dozen.

She was immediately admitted and a pulmonologist was consulted – the very same doctor who had witnessed the abscess miracle two years earlier. He looked at the CT results and confirmed that both her lungs were indeed, "full of PEs." But that wasn't all. There was evidence that every PE in her lungs, probably close to thirty, had all passed through her heart. And yet, there was no damage. None. And further, the clots had bypassed her brain.

What should have caused *both* a heart attack *and* a stroke, had ultimately caused neither.

During the subsequent eight-day hospital stay, Kailen began seeing a cardiovascular specialist who diagnosed her with a rare disorder called May-Thurner Syndrome (MTS). MTS is a condition of abnormal iliac vein compression that often results in swelling, pain, or clotting.

The specialist performed a series of three surgeries to help save Kailen's life: first, he placed a temporary inferior vena cava filter, or IVC filter, to protect her heart against any clots generated by the procedure; next, he used a medicine called tPA to dissolve the existing clots in Kailen's pelvis and lungs; then he placed a stent in the left common iliac vein.

Kailen was started on lifelong Coumadin therapy, a drug that thins the blood and protects against clotting. And it was at this point that she added two new doctors to her list – an adult gastroenterologist, for management of the ulcerative colitis (UC), and a hematologist, to direct her Coumadin therapy.

After the nightmarish week in the hospital, Kailen finished her senior year and enrolled at the University of Kentucky in the fall. Despite the UC limiting her sleep to less than three hours a night, college started off well for Kailen. She was taking a difficult course-load with the intention of applying to pharmacy school in a few years. But yet again, in September, Kailen's attempt at a normal life was stifled.

"Hey mama, whatcha doin'?"

Those were the words Kim heard, but the true message was hidden in Kailen's tone. Kim had heard it before and recognized it immediately – something was very wrong.

"Well, I think I might have another clot," Kailen said, her voice calm. "But don't worry, I'm with Kathryn and I'm laying really still."

Kailen *did* have another clot. When Kim and Jeff got her back to Baptist in Louisville, the iliac stent was completely clogged. Once again, the clot was massive, and this time it had caused some pretty significant damage. By the grace of God and the integrity of the stent, Kailen's heart and brain were safe. But the backflow of blood had severely damaged the valves in her legs. She would now have to wear compression stockings every day to keep her ankles from swelling.

Her cardiovascular specialist was brought back in and was able to dissolve the clots using the maximum amount of tPA allowed. When it came down to the final vial, he told the others in the room that if it didn't work, their only option would be to surgically remove the clot. Either that, or Kailen would likely die.

Those gathered around the operating table prayed, and with the final injection, the clot melted away and cleared the stent.

He also placed a permanent IVC filter. Kailen was clearly a high clot risk, even on the Coumadin, so he wasn't taking any chances. She was only eighteen, and now she had a stent in her hip, a filter in her heart, and medical stockings squeezing her legs.

Kailen had survived another blood clot but had missed almost two weeks of class. She was way behind, especially in her science courses, and the incessant exhaustion brought on by the ulcerative colitis was taking its toll. She wasn't sleeping and was losing copious amounts of blood through her stool, which was causing chronic anemia. By this point, she was getting monthly iron infusions and it still wasn't enough.

She had never failed at anything in her whole life, but that fall semester, she failed chemistry.

She was heartbroken. And she was angry. Her health

was getting in the way of everything. She went on and completed her freshman year, but things were getting worse. By the summer, she knew something had to change. She wouldn't be going back to UK in the fall.

In July, Kailen did a six-week steroid taper on top of her mesalamine therapy. The steroids caused her to gain water weight, her petite face becoming round in the cheeks. She was going to the bathroom more frequently and losing more blood than ever before; she didn't look or feel like herself. She had all but failed out of college. Depression was setting in.

Her journal entries became very dark. Her dreams were dying and all she could do was sit on the toilet and watch. Even the indomitable spirit gets bruised; even immutable joy sometimes grows quiet. Kailen was realizing she had endured eleven years of pain and agony, none of which she had done anything to deserve.

But Kim remembers Kailen's faith shining through, even in those darkest hours.

"The harder the physical things pressed in," Kim told me, "the more focused Kailen became on Jesus."

It was during that time, in the fall of 2009, that Kailen made one of her most famous proclamations. They were words that would define the rest of her life:

"I will not let my joy be stolen by troubles this world calls undeserved."

Reading that, it's easy to forget she was nineteen. There are many Christians that spend a lifetime in close relationship with Jesus and never develop that kind of faith. Kailen was rare, almost mythical at times – this gorgeous young woman made to do such hard things. But she wasn't a myth; she was a *person*. She experienced the same emotional undulations as every other human being on the planet. God didn't grant her immunity.

A few weeks after she got back from Mayo Clinic in Jacksonville, Kailen and Kim were sitting at home when Kailen finally aired out her deepest concern of all:

"Mama, how am I ever going to find someone? Who would ever want a body like this? I'm never going to find a man who has everything I want who actually wants me."

That was two weeks before we shook hands in the Southland Christian Church atrium.

As I mentioned before, Kailen was always meticulous. She also believed wholeheartedly in prayer. She had been praying for very specific things in her husband ever since she was a little girl. These things included tall, athletic, passionate about reading and writing, brown hair if possible, and of course, loves Jesus.

I don't know why, but God chose to give me those exact characteristics. And a few days after Kailen and I got engaged, I sat down with Kim at their kitchen table.

"I've been the carrier up to this point," she told me, referring to Kailen's health issues. "But now you are.

Even if you don't.

And I'm here to help as much or as little as you want me to."

I could see the fierce concern in her eyes, the fear that it was too much for me. I smiled and held her hand.

"Kim, there is nothing, and I mean *nothing,* that could ever tarnish your daughter's beauty in my eyes. As long as I have breath, I will guard her heart with my life."

She squeezed my hand, and I willingly accepted the weight.

♥ ♥ ♥

As summer faded to fall, Kailen slowly started lifting the veil.

She was still nervous, fearful I'd suddenly realize I didn't want my life to be like an episode of *House*, so I began taking steps to affirm my commitment. I learned her medication list and helped her remember to take them – something she was intentionally very bad about – and I researched her conditions.

I wanted to know what to do in case of emergency, but more than that, I wanted to build empathy. I wanted to love her better. The more I knew, the more I could anticipate her needs. Simple things, like quietly asking a waitress to seat us closer to the restrooms, turning up the volume on the TV if she had to hurry to the bathroom at home, or reminding her to do ankle pumps in the car so her feet wouldn't swell.

She was positively mortified when I started attending appointments. But despite her best attempts to push me away, I wasn't going anywhere. I held her hand as the cardiovascular specialist did another Doppler on her hip, ensuring the iliac stent was doing its job, and again a few weeks later as a nurse wheeled her back for a colonoscopy. The inflammation in Kailen's colon was so severe they weren't even able to complete the procedure.

I remember standing alongside Kim and Jeff as the doctor told us Kailen's ulcerative colitis was getting worse, and that it would be negligent not to act quickly. There were basically three options: one, continue mesalamine therapy with intermittent steroid tapers, which was commensurate with slapping a Band-Aid on a bullet hole. Two, consider total colectomy, a procedure to remove Kailen's colon and reroute her stool into an ostomy bag. Or three, initiate immunosuppressant therapy.

He said that word again – *Remicade* – but after a discussion with Kim and Jeff, we decided to pick option one, at least until after the wedding.

A total colectomy was Kailen's worst nightmare and the immunosuppressants were too dangerous. It was a painful stalemate, but we were eventually going to have to face it.

The week following the colonoscopy, I met a man who would change my life. We were at a hematology appointment and Kailen was getting her INR checked to make sure the Coumadin dose was appropriate. By this point I realized the medical community had essentially adopted Kailen. The nurses, the staff, the doctors – they all *adored* her. And I'd been admonished, on several occasions, that if I didn't take proper care of her, they knew a variety of ways to dispose of me.

But it was all fun and games until I met Dr. Patrick Williams.

Dr. Williams employed a process we now call extreme vetting. I was sitting in a chair beside Kailen, and Kim was across from me, laughing, as Williams offered a grueling assessment of my character. It *was* funny, looking back, but I can still see the iron-like focus in his eyes; part of him was kidding, but the other part – the larger part – was deathly serious.

As he stared me down, I remember thinking two distinct thoughts: one, who does this little Irish guy think he is? Dr. Williams stands about five-foot-seven and his nurses call him the "Little General." And two, I'm so thankful this man is Kailen's doctor.

When we stood to leave, he hugged Kailen, kissed her on the forehead, and told her to text him if she needed anything before her next appointment. I tried to slip out of the room without getting waterboarded, but he slapped a hand on my shoulder and squeezed.

Firmly.

He leaned in close and whispered, "I love that sweet girl with all my heart. And if you don't love her more than I do, you have no business being here. Do you understand?"

He suddenly seemed a lot taller than five-seven. "Yes sir," I told him. "I understand completely."

"*Good*," he said, slapping my shoulder again.

Though I didn't see it, I'm sure he was smiling as I scuttled into the hallway and grabbed Kailen's hand. The rest of the medical community viewed Kailen as an adopted child, but Dr. Williams saw her as one of his own. And I never would have fathomed, on that first day of interrogation, that five years later he would view me the same way.

On October 12th, I found out I had been accepted to the University of Kentucky College of Pharmacy. Kailen and I celebrated the achievement, then immediately decided to move our wedding up five months. We had initially planned on May, but getting married right before pharmacy school sounded like a recipe for a quick divorce.

Then there was the matter of Kailen's colon. Her bathroom visits hadn't increased in frequency, but they were getting more urgent. And more than once I had noticed the toilet bowl stained red with blood. If colectomy had to wait until after the wedding, maybe the wedding shouldn't wait quite so long.

Within a week, we had a date: December 18th, one year to the day from our first kiss.

That left us two months to get everything ready.

Wedding prep was hard on Kailen. Stress and lack of sleep pushed her body to the limit, and despite her vehement protests, she was forced back on steroids. She didn't finish the last taper until mid-December.

I can see her, walking down the aisle, cheeks puffy from prednisone, ankles swollen from damaged valves in her legs, and I remember realizing I'd never seen a more perfect living thing in all my life. There were no blemishes, no aberrations. In my eyes, she was flawless. God decided man wasn't fit to be alone, so he made woman. And it was *good.*

The ceremony went off without a hitch – minus the fact that I kissed her too soon, without the pastor's permission – and the reception was a veritable Combs-style celebration. I'm not normally a dancer, but K could persuade me to be just about anything and I twirled her around the room while our friends danced around us.

By eight o'clock, I'd had my fill. The event was fun and all, but I'd been waiting twenty-one years to consummate my marriage and I was ready to leave.

Unfortunately, when I hurried back over to the church to change clothes, I found one of my groomsmen had left a sex toy in my dress shoes. What he didn't realize, of course, was that Jeff wore the exact same shoes as me.

I'll say this: you haven't lived until you've been handed a vibrating condom by your newly-minted father-in-law. It's quite the experience.

I impatiently waited another hour while Kailen made her rounds, then we finally climbed in the Camry and left amid a raucous send-off. We spent our first married night at the Seelbach Hotel in downtown Louisville, then set out for our honeymoon in Gatlinburg the next morning.

Until our wedding night, the latest I had ever been with Kailen was two or three in the morning, so I truly had no idea what she dealt with. I didn't take an exact count, but that first night in Gatlinburg she must have gone to the bathroom at least twelve times. There was no way she slept more than two hours. It wasn't mathematically possible. And yet, the next morning, I rolled over to find her smiling unrestrainedly. And an hour later, we did a newlywed bee-bop all the way to the pancake house.

Our three days in Gatlinburg followed that motif – pancakes, a coffee-cup stroll through downtown, back to the room for consummation, then out for lunch, then consummation and possibly a nap, then out for dinner and some minor (and inexpensive) evening festivities.

One of my favorite nights was when we drove down to Pigeon Forge and stopped to rock-hop in a stream along the way. We explored for nearly an hour before Kailen found the perfect stone to take home to Jeff, who's amassed a rather impressive collection over the years. It was bright white and almost perfectly round, and though we couldn't have known it at the time, would eventually serve a very important, and *eternal*, purpose. (More on that later).

We were in dress clothes and were probably late to

our movie, but she was giggling as she bounced from boulder to boulder, the cold water running inches beneath her feet, her childlike joy echoing off the mountains. It was the one time we were glad to be honeymooning in Gatlinburg and not some exotic island like the rest of our friends. And when I say the one time, I do mean the *one* time.

The honeymoon ended and we went back to have Christmas with family. We spent Christmas Eve with Kailen's family in Louisville, then survived a tenacious blizzard on the way to Matanzas. It was a two-hour drive that took almost six; Kailen was asleep and I was bent white-knuckled over the steering wheel, very much awake and very much wondering why we hadn't stopped at a hotel before leaving civilization.

Four miles outside Leitchfield, a rural hamlet along the Western Kentucky Parkway, Kailen woke up and looked over at me. "I have to go to the bathroom," she told me.

"Ok, sweetie," I said. "We're not far from an exit. Maybe ten minutes or so."

She calmly shook her head. "I may not have ten minutes, babe."

I pried my white knuckles off the steering wheel and held her hand. There was a pressure point next to her thumb that sometimes helped alleviate the cramps. I massaged it for a while, and when it didn't help, I just held her hand and felt her squeeze every few seconds, as intestinal peristalsis rhythmically racked her body with pain.

Every time I pushed the accelerator, trying to hurry, the back end started to slide. There was at least five inches of fresh powder on the road. When I tried putting the car in low gear and gently increasing our speed, we ended up horizontal and very nearly hit the guardrail.

Never in the history of humanity has someone so badly wanted to get to Leitchfield, Kentucky.

We eventually made it, but Kailen didn't. She dug an extra pair of underwear out of her suitcase and bee-bopped through the snow into the gas station.

Helplessness is a feeling I've grown accustomed to by now, but it was fresh on that night and I cried sitting in the car by myself. My beloved, my darling among the maidens – she deserved better than to soil herself on the way to Christmas at her in-laws. She knew it, too, but there were no tears when she got back to the car. As always, she was smiling.

We didn't discuss it. I just wiped my eyes and she turned up the radio as we slid the Camry back onto the interstate.

Fifteen minutes later, she was already in pain again. All I could do was squeeze her hand and keep driving.

A few days after New Year's, our friends decided to take a ski trip. It was a Monday and we were all still out of school for Christmas break. All except Kailen.

She had decided not to go back to UK, a decision that secretly broke her heart, and instead opted to enroll at Spencerian College. She was in a certified medical assistant program and the course-load was much easier on her body. It was certainly a respectable path, but for Kailen, the girl that received a letter from the President of the United States in 8th grade, the class leader, the brilliant writer, the exemplary student, it fell short of her dreams.

She had her first day of class that Monday but excitedly told me to go on the trip. She knew I hadn't seen my friends in a while and some time away would reinvigorate me as a man. I was the sole married guy amongst a horde of bachelors, so admittedly I was mourning the loss of freedom and adventure. Once she gave me her blessing, it was an easy decision.

We all met at Ben's apartment. It was a big group – the Frankfort Crew plus a few – and as we were piling into vehicles, my phone rang.

I almost didn't answer it. I distinctly remember thinking I would just wait and call the person back when we stopped for gas. But then, for a reason I don't recall, I dug the phone out of my pocket.

It was Kim. "I just heard from the doctor's office," she told me. "Kailen's bloodwork came back and her potassium is critically-low. Bryan, they're saying she's in danger of having a heart attack."

I felt adrenaline surge as I walked back into Ben's apartment and sat on the stairs. Everyone else was still outside. "Do they want us to come in?" I asked.

"No, not yet. But they called in a prescription for her. Can you go pick it up?"

"Oh sure, no problem."

I was a dumb kid that didn't know anything about anything, so I was thinking our little skiing convoy could swing by the pharmacy then drop off the medication at Kailen's school on our way out of town.

That's what I was thinking, until Kim introduced me to reality.

"She can't be alone, Bryan. If she were to have any symptoms or chest pain or anything, you would need to get her to the ER immediately."

Ski trip – over. Freedom and adventure – *gone.*

I sat on the stairs and wondered how it was possible. I was twenty-two years old and couldn't go skiing with my friends because my wife might have a heart attack and die while I was gone. It was just a college ski trip, just a wintry January morning, but in truth it was much more: it was the morning I realized loving someone with your whole heart comes at a great cost.

It wasn't just a ski trip; it was symbolism. And as I stood in the parking lot, cold and alone, watching the convoy leave without me, it didn't feel like my friends were just driving away.

It felt like they were driving out of my life.

Even if you don't.

Bird-day breffust. That's how she said it.

When Kailen was little, Jeff says she sounded just like the rabbit from *Robin Hood.* Vestiges of that cute lisp had crept into adulthood and manifested in certain words and phrases. "Birthday breakfast" was one of those phrases, and it was also one of Kailen's favorite pastimes.

On her first birthday as a married woman, we did indeed have a birthday breakfast. I surprised her with Panera bagels and coffee in bed. The resultant squeal woke most of east Lexington and we danced around the room before realizing we were on the second floor and the people beneath us would likely be angry, then decided to keep dancing anyway.

That evening we went out to a fancy dinner. At that time, fancy wasn't an adjective often attributed to our lifestyle. As my Dad would say, "we barely had a pot to piss in." In reality, we had two pots to piss in and were grateful for them both, but the point is we were poor.

Which is why the generosity of a man named Ron Rager was so important.

I had met Ron the previous summer, a few weeks before Kailen and I got engaged. I was working the cash register at the pharmacy when he walked up. To be fair, I don't remember much about the encounter, but apparently it was memorable to Ron. Because ten minutes after he checked out and left the store, he came back in and waved me up to the counter.

Now, I worked at the Wal-Mart on Richmond Road

in Lexington. At Rich Road, if you got waved up to the counter, it could only mean one of two things: one, the patient took a few of their methadone in the parking lot and was coming back to claim you shorted them, or two, you're about to get stabbed. Sometimes, on nights and weekends, it might mean both. But thankfully Ron was just coming back in to say thank you.

"I appreciate good service," he told me, handing me his business card. I didn't look at it closely until after he left, but I did notice the BHG logo. Ron worked for Bluegrass Hospitality Group, the ownership entity for a large number of premier restaurants in Lexington.

"Anytime you and your girlfriend want a nice meal, you just call that number. I'm of the mind that quality service should be rewarded."

It was one of those rare interactions you remember the rest of your life. I don't remember Ron in the eidetic detail I often remember Kailen, but I do recall he was wearing a black suit with a gold tie and his voice sounded a lot like Walter White. We shook hands and I ardently thanked him. As he was walking out, I looked down at the card and realized Ron didn't just *work* for BHG, he was the chief operating officer.

So yeah, after a quick phone call to Ron, Kailen's birthday dinner was *fancy.* We walked into Malone's steakhouse liked we owned the place, took a seat in a gargantuan leather booth, and began basking in the land of milk and honey.

We didn't even order; the food just started coming.

Two appetizers, two wedge salads, followed by two heaping slabs of filet mignon drowning in shrimp. And just when I thought I might either vomit or develop gout, someone deposited half a chocolate cake on our table. We needed three to-go boxes the size of my head, but we weren't about to waste any of that delicatessen. We ate leftovers for a week.

When we got back home, I heard Kailen's phone ring. I'm not exactly sure where I was – probably the bathroom – but I remember her answering in her usual bubbly tone, then growing somber. I had been privy to enough "phone calls" by that point to know it was probably bad news and it was probably about Kailen's health.

It was. Her potassium was critical again. Only this time, it was worse.

The ulcerative colitis was completely out of control. Despite the mesalamines and frequent steroid tapers, Kailen was still using the bathroom close to twenty times a day. The fecal blood loss was rendering her perpetually anemic, but the bigger problem was the sheer loss of fluid, which was resulting in massive electrolyte depletion.

Her potassium, sodium, and iron were all disturbingly low, and for the second time in six months, a doctor told us that staying our current course was reckless and naïve. Kailen's life was in danger.

The next day, we were sitting in the doctor's office. It was time to revisit the stalemate. Kailen was hesitant to even consider total colectomy; the thought of having an ostomy bag for the rest of her life horrified her beyond description. As her husband, I continually affirmed her that all I cared about was her health and happiness. I wanted her to sleep through the night; I wanted her to feel good during the day; I wanted her to be able to go hiking or drive down the interstate without fear of incontinence. But more than all that, I wanted *her*. I wanted her to see me graduate; I wanted her to reach her dreams; I wanted to raise our children together and watch them grow. An ostomy bag was nothing in comparison to those things.

But Kailen was a beautiful twenty-one-year-old woman. She wanted all the same things I did, and just as badly, but she also wanted to feel pretty. She wanted to wear a bikini in the summertime and go running without fear the bag would burst open and poop would spill all over her.

A normal life.

That's all she wanted, and I wanted it for her.

So as tempted as I was to discourage the use of immunosuppressants, I forced myself to realize it wasn't *my* body I was bargaining with. It was Kailen's body, her colon, and thus, ultimately her decision. I would love and support her no matter what.

For the third time, we refused Remicade. Every immunosuppressant poses scary risks and side effects, but there was just something about Remicade that felt different. So even though the gastro continued to adamantly recommend it, we decided to go another way.

The back-up option was a drug called Imuran. Kailen began taking it in the spring of 2011, and by August, when I started pharmacy school, she weighed barely a hundred pounds.

Imuran was essentially poison. It lessened her bathroom frequency, but only slightly, and added dramatic appetite suppression and vomiting. My wife was emaciating right in front of me, and if we hadn't stopped it when we did, Imuran would have killed her.

"*Damn* immunosuppressants."

Those were the words of Dr. Patrick Williams. But we'll get to that later in the story.

In the shadow of all the health battles, it's easy to forget that Kailen and I were still a young couple. We weren't perfect people and our relationship was far from impenetrable. And though we didn't fight all that often, when our first real argument finally came, we made it count.

It happened on September 11th, 2011. I know because I remember thinking it was like the 9/11 of our marriage. It shook me in a way I had never been shaken before, and it nearly destroyed us.

One of Kailen's ex-boyfriends had treated her inappropriately during their relationship, and despite having deeply transparent conversations in pre-marital counseling, Kailen had decided to keep it from me. She later told me she chose to come out with it because she believed God would heal her if she trusted Him completely.

She *did* trust Him completely, but He didn't heal her.

He healed *me*.

I took the news pretty well initially. I hugged Kailen and apologized for her pain, even going so far as to tell her it wasn't a big deal and she didn't have to worry about me being upset. But in the days that followed, the fact that some guy had hurt my wife, and that she had lied to my face about it, threatened to consume me.

I'm justice-driven to the core, so in my twenty-two-year-old mind, something had to be done. I became obsessed with retribution to the point that I could think of nothing else, and soon decided I was going to introduce a little justice back into a flawed system. I was going to right the ship.

Two weeks later, after doing some research, I drove to where this guy worked. My intentions were far from platonic – I wanted to watch him bleed. I walked several laps around the store looking for him, and when I didn't find him, I hunted down a manager.

"Does such-and-such work today?" I asked.

The woman consulted the clipboard she was holding. "He's actually off tonight," she told me. "Do you want me to give him a message for you? He'll be in later this week."

Even if you don't.

Thank goodness he wasn't working. I don't think the College of Pharmacy would have appreciated an assault charge on my record, and I know Kailen wouldn't have. Such an act of careless violence would have damaged and likely ended our marriage.

By the grace of God, he had switched schedules due to a conflict. And after driving around town looking for his car, I eventually gave up my Wyatt Earp excursion.

I tell this story at my own expense, but I also tell it to illustrate a crucial point: God had to demolish my sense of justice and completely rebuild it. The road that lay ahead was wrought with unfairness the likes of which I couldn't even imagine, much less accept. So, He used Kailen's sweet innocence and honesty to begin a complete renovation of my worldview.

I had to humble myself and accept that He was sovereign, even in the midst of injustice – *especially* in the midst of injustice. I was not judge, jury, and executioner; in fact, I was none of the above. My only task was to follow God and trust Him, and while I wish I could say the process happened over night, it was a painful demolition and an arduous reconstruction.

It hurt, but I had already learned that God never wastes pain. He was preparing me, even then, for the greatest fight of my life.

♥ ♥ ♥

A month after I went on my manhunt, we were back at the doctor's office. The same look was in the doctor's eyes and the same sense of dread was draped over the room. Our options were down to two: total colectomy, or the drug-that-shall-not-be-named.

The doc gave us some informational handouts and we took another day or two to think it over. We were at Kim and Jeff's, sitting once again on those massive couches, and I remember scanning the sea of numbers listed on the package insert. As always, side effects were possible but unlikely, and according to the pharmaceutical company, the chances of a truly serious risk ever seeing fruition were less than a tenth of a percent.

Basically impossible, or at least that's what they want you to think, that way you'll buy their medication at $10,000-a-dose.

It only happens to those nameless, faceless folks all the ambulance-chasing lawyers recruit during soap opera commercial breaks. It doesn't actually happen to real people, right?

If that were true, big pharma wouldn't spend billions of dollars annually on their legal teams. The reality is, the percentages are small, but those percentages aren't numbers, they're people.

Unfortunately, the alternative also carried substantial risk. By this point, Kailen's condition was so advanced the doctor wasn't confident the integrity of her rectal tissue would ever support reattachment post-colectomy. That meant Kailen's worst fears were validated – an ostomy bag for life.

He didn't completely rule out the potential for

reattachment and a normal life after surgery, but he definitely cast significant doubt on the prospect.

That doubt was enough to convince us to play the odds.

Remicade.

Kailen began getting infusions in October 2011. Like Imuran, Remicade helped marginally. Her bathroom trips remained in double digits and she still wasn't sleeping, but unlike Imuran, Remicade didn't try to kill her immediately.

It waited until spring.

♥ ♥ ♥

Don't freak out.

It was early March, almost exactly a month before Kentucky beat Kansas to win the National Championship. I was sitting in class staring out the window at an angry sky when I felt my phone vibrate in my pocket. A massive storm front was moving in and it was starting to rain as I read the message.

Don't freak out, she'd written. *But I just almost died.*

There would eventually come a time when Kailen almost dying became borderline perfunctory, but in the spring of 2012, that time had not yet arrived. I did the only thing any sensible husband would in such a situation…I freaked out.

WHAT?!?!?!?!? I typed back.

She didn't reply for a few minutes and I was about to leave class to go call her when another message came through.

Yeah...I blacked out and fell in the floor. But everything's fine now. Dr. Williams is here. He thinks they were giving me the Remicade too fast. He called it anaphylactic shock.

I was just a measly first-year pharmacy student, but even I knew anaphylactic shock was serious. She quite literally almost died. As for the Dr. Williams part, I want to be clear that he was not the prescribing physician for Remicade. It just so happened the infusion center where Kailen received Remicade was also where Williams saw many of his chemotherapy patients. Lucky for us, he was nearby when Kailen hit the floor.

I texted back, *I'll be there in less than an hour.*

After I packed my things and left the classroom, Kim called me. She was already on her way to the infusion center and promised to keep me updated until I got there. She also informed me there were approximately nine confirmed tornadoes along the I-64 corridor, which is conveniently the only appreciable corridor linking Lexington to Louisville.

Twenty minutes later, I plunged into the storm like Bill Paxton in *Twister*.

The wind and rain pounded my two-wheel drive

Silverado, but I kept the accelerator pinned to the floor. It was a confluence of calamity, a Murphy-level conflagration. I was going nearly a hundred miles-an-hour when I exited 64 onto the Watterson Parkway, and by the time I slid into the hospital parking lot, all hell had officially broken loose: debris was flying across the pavement, street signs were doing backbends, and the rain wasn't so much falling as it was spraying, as though God had put his thumb over the end of the hose. It felt like a sea of needles pricking me as I ran into the building.

I hugged Kailen when I got to her room and found she was still hooked up to an IV. They had stopped the Remicade and started her on a combination of Benadryl and steroids to calm the allergic response. Her whole body was still flushed and I held her hand as she recounted the story.

She had been looking down at her phone when she suddenly developed tunnel vision; her heart pounded like a kick drum in her head. Realizing she was going to pass out, she reached for the call button. As fate would have it, the button had fallen beneath her chair. She couldn't reach it. So, she rolled into the floor, nearly tearing the IV line out of her arm, and crawled toward the door, hoping someone would see her before she passed out. A nurse came by seconds before Kailen lost consciousness and called for Dr. Williams.

It had been a very close call, *too* close, and we were all ready to get out of there. But just before Kailen's IV bag dripped empty, an alarm roared in the hallway.

A mob of nurses came running, helping patients out

of chairs and frantically rolling IV poles out of rooms. There was a tornado warning, someone explained. All patients had to be gathered in the basement. It was protocol.

Of course it is, I thought, seriously contemplating taking Kailen's IV out myself. But a nurse got to her first and we spent the next two hours in the basement of Norton Suburban Hospital.

When we finally got home, the conclusion was unspoken and undeniable – Remicade was done.

We had tried two immunosuppressants and both had failed miserably. Kailen had almost died, *twice*, and her colon wasn't any better. A cold reality was staring us in the face.

We were down to our last option.

The fall before we got married, Kailen and I adopted a dog – a tiny little boxer named Layla.

She was the runt of the litter, the smallest boxer any of us had ever seen, and we soon discovered she was more enigma than canine. She was nine months old when we got her, and less than an hour after bringing her home, she went into heat. Jeff bought diapers, cut a hole for her tail, and Layla pranced unashamedly around the house in a pair of Huggies.

Later that first night, we were in the floor playing with her when she honest-to-God started talking. It was more Kailen-language than actual English, but she got her point across.

She was incessantly quirky. For instance, she would only sleep if completely submerged beneath a blanket, head and all. She also wouldn't poop if you were looking at her. She'd glance up at you, as if you were the world's most despicable pervert, then prance off behind a tree and unload. We had never met an animal, or a person, or any living thing quite like her, and we instantly fell in love.

The summer after my first year of pharmacy school was spent in an ethereal state of Americana. Kailen was still very sick, and the thought of colectomy still lurked in the back of our minds, but somehow, during those long, steamy June and July days, we felt unshackled. It was like the heat had melted the weight away. It didn't matter that the relief was short-lived, it was still relief, and we planned to live in it while we could.

It was me, Kailen, and Layla – our little family crammed into our little apartment, living our quaint little life. We spent mornings sipping coffee and reading, then afternoons sitting by the pool. As the heat faded into cobalt twilight, we went on walks through Andover, the wealthy neighborhood next door, and dreamed about what life could be someday. I typically carried a tennis ball in my pocket and we'd stop at the park by the fire station on the way home and play fetch with Layla. She'd retrieve it twice, three times at the most, then lay down and begin ripping it to shreds.

I bought a lot of tennis balls that summer.

At night, we sat on the concrete steps outside our apartment and ate popsicles. The warm breeze pressed between the buildings and tousled Kailen's hair, making it dance on her shoulders. Her beauty was like the wind, fresh and reviving, and though you'd felt it a thousand times before, always unique. She was equal parts science and art, and those summer nights on the steps, licking popsicles, were her gallery.

Every night, I realized she could never be any more beautiful. And every morning, I realized I was wrong.

In the dog days of late July, we became obsessed with the Olympics. We watched it every night. I sat in my recliner with Layla in my lap and Kailen laid on the couch. She most always fell asleep, so I carried her to our room then came back out and either read or wrote until I too fell asleep. Those nights were mundane, but they were magic. For a little while, we were normal. We had a home and a family; we had a routine. We had dreams and popsicles.

But, like always, the normality was fleeting.

When August came and we both started back to school, the word "colectomy" started slowly finding its way into conversation. And to both of our surprise, it actually wasn't all that scary.

Kailen was sick and tired of being sick and tired and I was sick and tired for her. If a total colectomy could heal her, if it could give her life, if it could give us the future we dreamed about on our summer walks, then who cares about an ostomy bag.

Even if you don't.

We discussed it with Kim and Jeff and began making tentative plans to have the surgery over Christmas break. We would do it at Mayo Clinic in Rochester, Minnesota, where the world's leading colorectal surgeon was employed. We were actually beginning to feel tendrils of excitement about the possibilities.

But then Sunday came – August 26th, 2012.

We were getting ready for church when Kailen finally showed me what she'd found a few days prior. She had been praying it would just go away, so she'd waited to tell me. But when it got larger instead of smaller, she had no choice.

She had on a light blue blouse, white capris, and brown sandals. Her hair was impeccably straight and longer than it had ever been. She was breathtaking.

Everything about her was perfect. Everything except the lump in her left breast.

We didn't tell anyone right away. I suspect Kailen told Kim, and Kim told Jeff, but outside of that, the secret was sealed inside our apartment.

Kailen and I got on our knees that Sunday afternoon and started praying. I laid hands on her morning and night; we fasted all week. I pleaded with God to just make it disappear, to let us go back to a life where our biggest concern was whether Kailen would have an ostomy bag. But by Friday morning, the lump hadn't budged. If anything, it was bigger.

Kailen missed class that Friday and drove to Louisville for an appointment with her primary care doctor. He wasn't in, so she saw his PA. When she got back to her parents' house and Kim asked how things went, Kailen said the appointment had gone well but confessed she hadn't asked about the lump.

Though she claimed she had forgotten, we all knew it was intentional; she was afraid of what the answer might be. We all were.

Kim was giving piano lessons to a church friend's daughter at the time, and the friend happened to be a pediatrician. So when the day's lesson was over, Kim asked her friend to take a look at the lump.

Though the pediatrician wasn't terribly concerned after performing the impromptu breast exam, she was concerned enough to refer us to one of her colleagues, a radiologist at Baptist Health that specialized in breast care.

The radiologist got us in quickly and we headed to Baptist the next morning, the Saturday before Labor Day. Kim went back with Kailen while Jeff and I sat in the waiting room and read outdoor magazines in an effort to calm our nerves.

About thirty minutes later, Kim came and got us. She was smiling and the mood was relatively lighthearted as we made our way through the labyrinth of hallways that comprised the radiology department.

Even if you don't.

I was still anxious, but inwardly I breathed a sigh of relief.

When we finally made it to the exam room, Kailen was gowned and sitting on a table. The radiologist was nice and took time to give us a detailed explanation. He had done a full breast exam and had also imaged the lump. It was large and well-formed, which we already knew, but overall he wasn't worried.

The lump did, however, meet two of the three criteria he used to determine the need for biopsy, so he made an appointment for Kailen to come back the following week.

The biopsy was more or less a formality, he explained. He placed the odds of malignancy right around 6%. *Six out of a hundred.* His rationale made sense and he spoke with confidence, but something didn't feel right. That 6% reminded me of another very small percentage I had seen recently, buried in the fine print of a medication package insert.

Nonetheless, we continued to pray. We stayed in Louisville that Sunday and went to church with Kim and Jeff, then spent a leisurely afternoon watching sports. By the time we drove back to Lexington, we were both feeling better. Our apartment imbued a sense of comfort, as did re-immersion in our daily routine. We went to class, we studied, we walked Layla at night. It felt like life was back on track, like the cancer scare was fading quietly into the rearview.

Kailen went for the biopsy as scheduled, and despite hurting like hellfire – imagine having a six-inch needle shoved all the way through your boob – the day went smoothly. She was back home that night and made a delicious dinner. We talked about the biopsy, but only briefly. Beyond that, we just prayed and tried to live life normally.

Nothing happened. For almost twenty-four hours, we heard nothing. I'd be lying if I said we weren't somewhat haunted by that 6% chance, but we were confident God wouldn't allow it to happen. Kailen had already been through so much. There was no way God was going to pile cancer onto an already-full plate.

We prayed, we trusted, we kept going.

Then, on Thursday, September 13th, there was a knock at the door. I had block exams the next day and was sitting at my desk, studying, while Kailen watched Food Network in the bedroom. I was only mildly curious when I first stood up, but as I walked to the door, I started getting nauseous.

It wasn't exactly a premonition, but I certainly felt impending doom.

I looked through the peephole and knew immediately.

It was Kim and Jeff, and Kim was teary-eyed. I opened the door, feeling like I might vomit, and Kim wrapped her arms around me. I wanted to hug her back but couldn't seem to move; the shock had paralyzed me. So I just stood there and felt her warm tears stream down my neck.

Even if you don't.

Kailen had heard the commotion and walked into the living room. I remember standing in the space between her and her parents; I don't recall why, but I was standing in the middle all by myself, on an emotional island, looking back and forth between the shores.

"Kailen, sweetie…" Kim began, then paused before stating the obvious.

Time stood still as I watched Kailen's reaction. She wore black yoga pants, an orange t-shirt, and had the same look in her eyes as the night she told me she was made to do hard things. It was almost like she'd been expecting it, narrowing her eyes at me as if to say, "I warned you."

Then she laughed. You don't believe me, but I swear on my life she did.

It would become her battle mantra: *laugh first, cry later.*

Here's the experience in her own words (taken from TeamKCT blog post, September 13th, 2013):

> *"Just like I never want to forget what happened on September 11th, 2001, I never want to forget the reality of September 13th, 2012.*
>
> *Where was I on that day? I was at home, in Lexington, going about a normal day. I was expecting to get normal results from my biopsy at any moment.*
>
> *What was I doing? I was cooking dinner and*

helping Bryan in any way I could as he was preparing for his first set of blocks in his second year of pharmacy school. I, myself, was between quarters of classes and about to start my externships at the end of the month. That was my last step before being able to become a certified medical assistant with phlebotomy. We were also ready for colon removal, and once that was over, we were both very excited about being so close to a normal life.

Who was I with? Bryan and I were home alone when we heard a knock on our door. We both looked at each other since we weren't expecting company but I didn't think anything of it. Bryan, however, immediately got a funny look on his face. We opened the door to see both my parents standing there. Dad with a look I'd never seen before and mom with old tears on her face and new tears ready to fall at any moment. They came in and all I can remember is mom saying, "It's cancer," and then everyone was hugging me.

How did I feel? Oddly enough, the first thing I did was laugh. I don't know how to explain it without going into great detail, but I knew it was going to happen. God had actually been preparing my heart and mind for years so when it came to be, I just laughed. I never spoke of it; I never wanted cancer. I prayed to never have cancer, and I never accepted it. But some part of me somehow knew it was coming. So I laughed.

Even if you don't.

Here I was, so close to finally being colon-free and working a real job. And suddenly it was gone. So close to having freedom from health complications and able to go and do whatever I wanted. And suddenly it was gone. SO close to feeling normal and like what I had always imagined your typical 22-year-old would feel like. And suddenly it was gone. We were so, so close and now all of a sudden I had colon disease AND breast cancer.

So all I could do was laugh.

"Invasive ductal carcinoma with lobular features."

Dr. Williams said the words, his enunciation flawless, and though Kailen and I heard them come through the phone, they sort of clanked off our ears like Shaq shooting a free throw.

Dr. Williams was Kailen's hematologist, and now he was also her oncologist. He had already scheduled a brain MRI and PET scan for the following day. He prayed with us, promised to see us tomorrow, and clicked off.

We were in the living room of our apartment, Kim and Jeff on the couch, Kailen sitting in my lap in the recliner. Layla knew something was wrong and was laying at my feet as opposed to buried beneath a blanket somewhere.

We were the same little family in the same little

apartment, but now we were up against a mighty foe.

Summer's sweet relief was a distant memory.

Kim and Jeff stayed with us that night, but they left for a while to give us time alone. The apartment was incredibly quiet, a sort of dense, asphyxiating silence, and the setting sun bathed the room in amber. We could have yelled and screamed and poured out our anger at God, and maybe we should have, but we didn't. I just held Kailen in my arms, smelled the floral-scent of her hair, felt her heartbeat strong and true against my chest, and silently begged God not to take her away.

When Kim and Jeff got back, a plan had been formed. They would get Kailen to her appointments the next day while I stayed in Lexington and took my exams. One of the abiding joys of pharmacy school block exams is that you take them on Friday, Saturday, and Monday. Makes for quite a weekend, even if your wife *wasn't* just diagnosed with cancer. As it stood, I would finish Friday exams then come pick Kailen up in Louisville.

An hour or two later, after we all tried and failed to eat dinner, I took my first step along the journey that would eventually callous my soul: I went back into my office and closed the door.

Everyone was still awake and firmly entrenched in a state of shock, but I had a nasty endocrinology exam the next morning at 8 AM. I had no choice but to swallow my tears and study.

At some point, much later, Ben and Erin heard the

news and came by to see us. They were only there a short time and I don't remember many details, but I greatly appreciated their thoughtfulness. They had just come from a flag football game and they smelled like grass and sweat and youthfulness. They were still kids, and as of five hours prior, I *wasn't*.

Nothing ushers in adulthood like war.

That night I went to bed around two or three but didn't do much sleeping. I tossed and turned, held Kailen, and intermittently forced vomit back into my stomach. By dawn, I had regurgitated enough acid to lightly singe the full length of my esophagus and sat up thinking this must be what a hangover feels like. Then I rolled over and held Kailen a little longer and wished our life was different.

Ten minutes later, my alarm went off and I stumbled groggily into the shower. By the time I got ready for class, Kim and Jeff were up stirring around but Kailen was still lying in bed. I gently kissed her lips then got on my knees and prayed.

I continued praying all the way to school. I had been a Christian since I was twelve years old. I believed in Jesus and I believed that He healed people. So, I asked Him. Over and over again. As I got on the bus at K-Lot, as I walked into the College of Pharmacy, as I sat down at my desk – I just kept asking, "*Jesus, please heal Kailen.*"

But as exams were passed out and I started bubbling in my scantron, a single thought was recurrent in my brain. I tried to suppress it, tried to force it back down, but like the acidic bile from the night before, it wouldn't stay. It kept coming back up, singeing my soul with its acridness.

Even as I turned in my exam, it was still there, like an echo from a bad dream. That horribly ineluctable fact was all I could think about.

My wife has cancer.

With Saturday came an irrational optimism.

Nothing had changed – Kailen had a cancerous lump in her left breast, we still had no results from the brain MRI or the PET scan, and I had three exams in the span of six hours. But inexplicably, as I watched the sun rise over campus, I felt an overwhelming sense of God's sovereignty. He had knit Kailen together in the womb; cancer was nothing for Him. If He was on our side, what was there to worry about?

My Saturday exams were tough, but I drove home awash in that same optimism, indescribably certain that everything was going to be okay.

Kailen was experiencing the same thing. When I got back, we literally danced in the kitchen. *Danced.* We laughed as we made lunch, then sat and watched football all afternoon.

"This has a purpose," she told me, leaning against my chest. "This is no different than the blood clots or the abscess in my lung. God is good, and He's my healer. He's going to turn this pain into something beautiful. So, I suppose, cancer can go ahead and bring it on."

Kailen breathed the same oxygen as you and me; she lived inside this world just like the rest of us. But she wasn't *of* it. She was a heavenly diaspora. I've often hypothesized that the world treated her much like our bodies treat an infection – it walled her off and did everything in its power to destroy her. To the world, the devil's domain, Kailen was non-self, a dangerous threat to be contained and quelled.

The next morning, she went to hear Jarrod sing at church while I stayed home and studied. Shortly after she got back, I got an email about my endocrinology exam: I had scored 100%. As in, I didn't miss a single question. It was like God patting me on the back, affirming my faith and encouraging me to keep at it. Our optimism, it seemed, was paying off.

I finished my exams on Monday and the week passed with seductive tranquility. No more perfect scores, but I had performed well on my tests, and most importantly, Kailen was feeling good. Her colon was abnormally cooperative, and despite looming over us like a dark cloud, the cancer was beginning to seem more and more impotent.

We caught it early, we thought. *Just a little lump,* we thought. *They'll cut it out and we'll move on with life,* we thought.

We thought all those things, until around four o'clock Sunday afternoon.

We were lying in bed watching one of Kailen's favorite cooking shows when her cell phone rang. And if you haven't noticed by now, in this story, a ringing cell phone is often a harbinger for tragedy.

"It's Dr. Williams," she whispered, then scurried into the living room and closed the bedroom door. I could hear her voice every now and then, filtering through the wall, but mostly what I heard was silence. I laid face down and begged God He was once again patting us on the back, affirming our faith, encouraging us to keep at it.

But He wasn't. Not this time.

When she came back, she wasn't crying. There were no tears. But there was an emotion in her eyes I had never seen there before – *fear.* For the first time in the three years I'd known her, Kailen was genuinely afraid.

She sat her notebook on the bed. She had taken copious notes and I skimmed through them until I reached the final line:

Very bad, she'd written, and underlined it three times.

The brain MRI was clean, but the PET had revealed hypermetabolic activity in several places throughout Kailen's body. It was all contained to bony tissue, which Williams explained was favorable as far as prognosis was concerned, but overall the results were, as Kailen had put it, *very bad.*

We would need a bone biopsy to officially confirm

the diagnosis. But Williams already knew the truth and so did we: the cancer was stage IV, the most advanced stage possible.

A stage IV diagnosis means the cancer has metastasized from the primary site, traveled through the body, and taken up residence in a distant organ. It means the cancer can still be treated but can no longer be cured. It will never go away. Not completely.

Which means, eventually, it will kill its host.

It was the first time I'd ever felt betrayed by God. What about Him being good? What happened to Him being Kailen's healer? What about that stupid optimism we felt?

Nothing in all the world hurts more than false hope. I learned that lesson the hard way, on the first Sunday of autumn, when I asked God for a pat on the back and He gave us a death sentence instead.

As shock slowly turned to grief, Layla jumped onto the bed, I pulled Kailen tight against me, and together, our little family wept.

Around midnight, long after Kailen and Layla were both sound asleep, I crawled out of bed, brewed a pot of coffee, and went back to my office to prepare for class on Monday.

Because even stage IV cancer can't stop the dawn.

Part Three

The War

"War is hell."

-General William Tecumseh Sherman

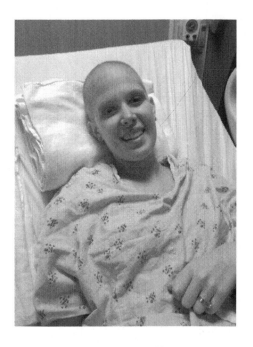

The next week was like boarding up a beach house: You know the hurricane's coming, but you can't appreciate the true violence of the thing until it actually arrives.

It began at a small round table in Dr. Williams' office. Kailen and I, along with both our parents, were crammed into the tight space, hanging on to every word

Williams had to say. It felt like the moment at the end of the gladiator games, when Caesar holds his thumb sideways and playfully deliberates the warrior's fate.

It may have felt like that, but it wasn't like that.

Williams wasn't playing, and our fate was already decided.

He calmly explained the plan: chemotherapy would start immediately after diagnostic testing and would be followed by extensive radiation. He gave us insight as to what this might look and feel like, and tried his best to be encouraging without outright lying to us.

He always had a gentle honesty about him. He didn't sugarcoat, but he also didn't hit you over the head with a shovel of truth. Nonetheless, he made it clear that remission was our objective. The word "cure" was no longer part of our battle vocabulary.

When he finished answering our onslaught of questions, he told us each to grab a hand. We locked hands all the way around the table as he led the room in prayer, sincerely petitioning the Lord for Kailen's healing and for a divine allotment of strength and endurance for me. There wasn't a dry eye in the place, including his.

After our parents stepped into the hallway, Dr. Williams pulled me and Kailen aside. His eyes were red-rimmed, but his voice was stern. "You've watched movies and read books and seen shirts and bumper stickers with all kinds of cute little sayings. 'Fight Like a Girl,' 'Save the Ta-Tas,' and the like, which is all well and good." He placed a hand on each of our shoulders. "But this is war. It's going to be brutal for a while. Make no mistake, you're in a fight for your lives. Staying alive is a conscious choice you'll have to make, and it won't always be preferable. But I can promise you one thing – I'll fight alongside you every step of the way."

Kailen took a deep breath and nodded. "I'm ready."

The next day, Kailen began a battery of medical testing while I had the distinct pleasure of going back to class.

I was oh-so-ironically beginning my cancer therapeutics block, which meant I spent my days listening to my abstrusely brilliant and exceedingly accomplished professors repeatedly tell me that:

1) Chemotherapy is a barbaric poison and 2) Maybe one of you will come up with something better one day (cue the condescending laughter) and 3) Statistically speaking, stage IV breast cancer patients are unlikely to live five years beyond diagnosis.

My days were tough, but Kailen's were far worse. That week she had a bone biopsy of the metastasis in her C7 vertebrae – a procedure in which she was laid on a table and someone dug out literal chunks of her spine – a pelvic and spinal MRI, a biopsy of the other breast (a replay of the "needle through the boob" episode), and finally, a PowerPort jammed into her subclavian vein.

The PowerPort, also known as a port-a-cath, provided quick intravenous access, which was crucial considering Kailen had miniscule veins and would be requiring frequent infusions. The procedure was performed outpatient, and while we waited in recovery, the surgeon said something formative.

She told me, "You have great equanimity."

As a lover of words, I was impressed. But the lasting resonance had far deeper roots.

"That's critical," she added, nodding at Kailen, who was still sedated. "Because she'll feed off your emotion. Many days will be horrible and full of emotional crests and troughs, but when she gets home you have to be her rock, her one steady place of refuge. The stronger you are, the stronger she'll be. And the stronger she is, the longer she'll live."

Equanimity. It was an art I intended to master.

Monday, October 1st, was dubbed "Haircutting Day." Alex Weires kindly came over and did a photo shoot prior to Kailen's haircut, effectively capturing her youthful beauty and her long, flowing locks.

Kailen had strikingly gorgeous hair, so watching the strands that had once danced on her shoulders slowly sway to the floor was heart-wrenching.

As it piled at her feet, I thought of how she was superior to Sampson; the loss of his magnificent hair had cost him his strength, but Kailen was actually made stronger by her loss, somehow emboldened by the injustice. The words the NICU doctor said on the first night of her life were still ringing true: *"She's a fighter, and she's got one helluva temper."*

Her pixie cut lacked the elegance of her former look, but it was impossibly cute and she embraced it without hesitation. She also embraced my bald head, which was not cute, but rather looked more like a topographical map of Utah. It made Kailen feel loved and special and supported, so I displayed my unflatteringly mountainous skeletal anatomy proudly.

She had her first chemo infusion the next day, October 2nd. The drug was Taxotere, a mainstay in the treatment of breast cancer; she would be starting a "3-week on, 1-week off" regimen.

Ideally, the treatment would last six months. But as you'll soon discover, our circumstances were rarely ideal.

On Friday, October 5th, Kailen was back in Lexington recovering from her first chemo and I was doing my best to stay awake in Pharmacy Law. She had texted me before class and told me she was feeling okay, just really tired. No vomiting yet, for which we both praised God.

Pharmacy Law was just as boring as you might imagine, and by the time it ended, the class breathed a collective sigh, yearning for the weekend to start. Because of Kailen's health struggles, I had spent very little time getting to know my classmates. I was close with the five guys I sat with – we called ourselves *The Row C Alliance* – but beyond that, I barely knew anyone. I knew most of their names, but little else.

Which made what happened next all the more meaningful.

As I gathered my things and said bye to The Row C Alliance, I noticed people starting to gather at the front of the classroom. It wasn't altogether strange for a handful of folks to congregate around the professor, asking questions or begging for mercy, but on that morning, it was much more than a handful.

All of a sudden, the entire class was standing up front, and I felt my friend, Matt Scherrer, pat me on the back.

"We're with you, buddy," he said.

And it hit me all at once.

People were taking off sweatshirts and jackets, revealing pink T-shirts underneath. Everyone. Every single person. They all had on a pink t-shirt with the words "Team KCT" written in white letters across the chest.

Our class president, Chris Terry, waved me up front and showed me the basket the class had assembled for me and Kailen. There were dozens of cards, books, notes of encouragement, and handheld games like Tetris and Yahtzee that Kailen could play while getting her infusions. I was overwhelmed, pleasantly smothered by the gratuitous generosity of strangers.

When I got home, Kailen and I discovered the cards contained more than $500 in gift cards to restaurants, gas stations, movie theaters, and nail salons.

As Kailen continued opening envelopes and reading the personal messages inscribed inside the books, I sat on the bed and looked out at the weeping willow in our backyard. Its lanky branches coiled and unfurled with the autumn breeze, and as I watched them tango, I wondered how a group of strangers had managed to make us feel so loved.

As the hurricane formally came ashore and began wreaking havoc, Kailen and I established a new normal.

Her body was steadily emaciating, becoming sallow in the cheeks, hips, and ribcage, and her flawless tan skin was slowly fading to a sickly gray-green pallor. By Halloween, her pixie cut was falling out in clumps, coating her pillowcase and clogging drains. The chemo was ruthlessly ravaging her body, but in hopes it was also ravaging the cancer, we kept at it.

Her infusions were typically on Monday morning, so I drove her to Frankfort to meet her parents on Sunday night. There's a Starbucks right off the exit that served as our rendezvous point, and for twenty minutes every Sunday evening, we would sip coffee and pretend to be a normal couple out on a date.

It didn't occur to me until much later that the Frankfort Starbucks – the halfway point between our apartment in Lexington and the infusion center in Louisville – was yet another emotional island, much like the one I'd stood on in our living room the night we found out the lump was malignant.

It was a brief purgatory, an alluring mirage. It was a physical manifestation of false hope.

We buzzed Kailen's head on Halloween night and by mid-November there was nothing left but peach fuzz. We were blessed that she was mostly spared from the voracious nausea many cancer patients deal with, but when the chemo reached her colon, it was commensurate with tossing kerosene on a bonfire.

By Christmas break, Kailen was using the bathroom close to thirty times a day. She had barely any appetite and the dozens of pills she was taking – for pain, nausea, and ulcerative colitis – weren't helping matters. She was losing precipitous amounts of weight, and Dr. Williams was concerned.

The weight loss and malnutrition were hindering her body's ability to fight the cancer, he explained. It was going to affect prognosis. Something had to be done.

He gave us the name of Louisville's best colorectal surgeon and we started doing our research. There were several accomplished surgeons in the area, some of whom had performed thousands of colectomy procedures, but we soon discovered the complexity of Kailen's case made even the most experienced surgeons nervous.

Considering the stakes, we weren't taking any chances. So, the following week, Dr. Williams called in a favor.

Soon thereafter, Kailen was accepted at Mayo Clinic in Rochester, Minnesota, a facility that specializes in complexity. Though she was still mortified by the thought of having an ostomy, the game had changed; this was now life or death.

Thanks to Dr. Williams' connections at Mayo, we would not only be getting a GI consult, but would also be seeing an oncologist and a breast surgeon to discuss long term treatment options. We were excited, if it's possible to be excited about such a thing, and began preparing ourselves for a trip to Minnesota.

There was just one small problem: We had no money.

Even if you don't.

Which is where Team KCT first exerted its weight.

When word spread that Kailen would be heading to Mayo, unsolicited donations started pouring in. A formal gala benefit was also organized, which raised thousands of dollars toward health and travel expenses. And I won't mention his name here because I know he wouldn't want the recognition, but a benefactor from a local church offered to pay for all flight and hotel expenses, not only for the first trip, but for any future trips as well.

The magnanimity of that benefactor, of our friends and family, and of complete strangers, made healing a possibility. And for that, a simple *thank you* would never be adequate.

On January 7th, the day of Kailen's tenth chemo infusion, she tweeted: *"It's a new year with a renewed faith for the healing and restoration soon to come."*

Two months later, on March 11th, as our flight to Rochester lifted off the runway, Kailen and I looked out and thought we saw that healing and restoration painted across the northern horizon.

But we were wrong.

It was just another mirage.

Rochester reminded me of a miniature Lexington, only instead of being centered around a university, it was centered around a hospital.

Mayo Clinic is a magnificently foreboding series of Mordorian structures, composed of gunmetal gray steel. Downtown is quaint and full of character, and clings tightly to the Clinic as its source of life.

The Rochester airport, however, was tiny and decidedly rural, built in the middle of farmland some twenty miles outside town. We took a long cab ride to our hotel and got settled in before having dinner at a restaurant called The Canadian Honker.

No matter how dire the circumstances, Jeff always worked diligently to amplify simple pleasures. It was no different on that first evening at Mayo, when we ate like kings at a restaurant named after a goose, or the next morning when he arrived at my and Kailen's room with fresh Caribou Coffee and pastries.

Our first day at the Clinic began just after daybreak and continued well into the afternoon. That night, back at the hotel, Kailen wrote her first TeamKCT blog post.

Here's an excerpt from the day one summary (March 12th, 2013):

> *My first appointment was at 6:45 AM. We arrived at the clinic at 6:26 and got to gather with other patients and watch as the doors opened at 6:30. After a quick registration, and a little look-see around the immaculately pristine lobby and foyer, we headed up to start the day by seeing an oncologist/hematologist and breast surgeon.*
>
> *Our first appointment was with the*

Even if you don't.

oncologist and we had to wait a good while before being seen. Apparently, the number of medical charts I have acquired over my life is extensive even for a Mayo patient. All the doctors were quite impressed which made me wonder whether I should be proud of myself or depressed...just kidding. But it did take them a good while to look through my history before coming to see me.

We spoke with a Fellow first and were immediately reminded of why we love Mayo so much. She was very impressive and quickly put us at ease as we became more and more assured of how well she and the other doctors were already grasping the complexity of my case.

We then spoke with the doctor and she was wonderful. She seemed to fully understand where we have been, how we are feeling now, and helped show us options to decide where we want to go from here.

Coming to Mayo, we knew the cancer was obviously very important, but because of how poor my quality of life is right now, everything appears to be headed toward colon removal sooner rather than later. And that is exactly what I was praying for! I am so chained down by ulcerative colitis that once it's gone I will be able to not only have more of a life, but I'll be able to battle cancer even harder and kick its butt for good!

...So, day one of my Mayo adventure is down

and while I'm exhausted, I could not be more thrilled to be here. I thank God for going before me and preparing the right doctors for us and making sure I can be seen by the right people at the right time. And I pray that will be the case for the rest of my stay!

Thank you again and again to you ALL for your support, your financial blessings, your texts, and your many prayers!... My situation is not ideal by any means, but I will be forever thankful for how it has allowed me to appreciate and love in a deeper way.

The next morning, appointments didn't start as early and the day didn't last as long. We met with a gastroenterologist who seemed to grasp Kailen's case with effortless brilliance. She took him through her health journey, starting at age eleven, and he barely took notes. At the end, he assured us we had done everything we could and it was definitely time to consider surgery. He scheduled a number of consults and imaging appointments for the next day and told us to go enjoy the afternoon.

We took his advice. We spent several hours perusing downtown, checking out local restaurants, shops, and discovering what Kailen called "hidden treasures." We ate at a café, then bought coffee and eventually stumbled upon our favorite place in Rochester – Barnes and Noble.

I know you're probably thinking we could go to Barnes and Noble in just about any major city in America, but this one was different.

This Barnes and Noble occupied the Chateau Theater, which first opened its doors as a vaudeville house in 1927. The cornerstone was laid by Dr. Charles Mayo himself. With its Art Deco exterior, along with deep blue, star-filled ceilings, walls meant to emulate a medieval French village, and numerous castle turrets shrouding a prominent proscenium arch, the Chateau Theater was just as magical to us as it had been to movie-goers in the 30's and 40's. In 1980, it was adopted into the National Register of Historic Places.

So no, this wasn't just any Barnes and Noble. It was like God had placed it in our path for the sheer pleasure of it, a token of assurance that He was still with us.

All of downtown Rochester was charming and we thoroughly enjoyed our exploration. We had no way of knowing, however, that the chic cafes and boutiques, and of course, the bookstore, would eventually become like a second home to us.

The following day was packed full of imaging studies and scans, and around 4 o'clock, we finally settled into an appointment with the surgeon. From our research, we knew this man was one of the world's leading colorectal surgeons; seeing him in the flesh was sort of surreal. Having him review Kailen's chart and consider us for surgery was like asking Rembrandt for a caricature.

He was wearing a suit, but his demeanor was surprisingly relaxed. We gathered around him and the first thing he said was, "There's absolutely no reason for you to live this way."

We all kind of looked at each other, unsure of what he meant.

"You're so young and have been through so much," he said. "I'm sorry for all you're enduring. But your sick colon should no longer have any part in your suffering."

Kim was the first to verbalize the question we were all thinking: "So...surgery *is* possible?"

"Oh sure," he replied with a shrug. "I'm going to do it."

I glanced over at Kailen, who was crying and smiling at the same time, then looked back at the doctor and asked, "When?"

He shrugged again. "Have you eaten since noon?"

Kailen told him she hadn't.

"Then we'll do it tomorrow. Stay NPO overnight and be at Rochester Methodist around 6:30 tomorrow morning."

The air suddenly left the room. Kailen would later describe the moment this way (taken from TeamKCT blog post, March 15th, 2013):

> *The Taylor/Combs clan immediately exhaled, felt a weight lift off, and all of us began to tear up. It was the moment we had been dreaming of for so long, and now we were in it.*

Even if you don't.

After twelve years of agony, Kailen's colon bondage was almost over.

♥ ♥ ♥

Kailen woke up laughing on the morning of March 15th. It was not normal behavior for someone about to have a major organ cut out of their abdomen, but Kailen wasn't normal, and this particular organ was a real pain in the behind.

As we walked into Rochester Methodist and began registration, she wrote these words: *"New life begins and chains are broken."*

She had been shackled by ulcerative colitis for over half her life, bound to the bathroom, stifled by insecurity, tethered to the quickest route to a toilet. She had bled and cramped and suffered from diarrhea every day for a decade. And now, the chains were coming off. She was breaking free, with plans of using her newfound freedom to beat stage IV cancer.

During surgery prep, there was a complete absence of anxiety. Not only for Kailen, but for all of us. We had a bounce in our step, an abiding peace galvanizing our resolve. Kim used the blog to give surgery updates and she described the experience this way (taken from TeamKCT blog post, March 15th, 2013):

> *She was so ready to get things going this morning...no fear or anxiety, just excitement. This has been such a long road with twists and turns we certainly never expected or would have chosen. How thankful we are for God's*

faithfulness and promises to never leave us! His Presence is so tangibly here with us and so incredibly evident in Kailen's countenance and courage.

By mid-afternoon, it was done. According to the surgeon – let's just call him Rembrandt from now on – it was a textbook procedure. When they wheeled Kailen into the hospital room, we clapped and cheered and I did a little hip gyration which made Kailen laugh which made her abdomen hurt which earned me an elbow to the ribs from Kim.

Kailen was certainly sore, and definitely drugged, but she was mostly smiling and we spent the rest of that afternoon and evening attending to her needs and keeping her entertained.

A nurse came by and showed us how to properly empty the ileostomy bag now attached to Kailen's stomach. She didn't like the bag; in fact, she hated it. But her immense gratitude transcended every other emotion, and I never once – *never* – heard her complain.

Kim and Jeff left late, close to midnight, and I settled into one of those beloved hospital couch-beds that are more conducive to scoliosis than sleep. I then woke up less than an hour later to alarms blaring.

It was a tough night, or rather, as we would come to understand, a relatively normal night in the hospital.

There are no tough nights in the hospital in the same way there were no bloody days at Gettysburg. There are merely nights; they're all tough, they're all bloody, and they all suck.

Kailen battled horrific nausea all night, and vomiting only served to amplify the pain in her abdomen. At one point, her heart rate was up, her blood pressure was down, her urine output completely stopped, and both IV pumps quit working.

As I said, it was a night in the hospital.

Rembrandt came by early the next morning and gave us some shocking news: Kailen never actually had ulcerative colitis. Based on the flex sigmoidoscopy he performed prior to the procedure, along with pathology reports and surgical observations, he was confident the diagnosis was Crohn's Disease.

He showed us pictures of her colon to help illustrate his point, but I could no longer pay attention to what he was saying. I was transfixed by the macabre images. Her colon looked like it had been used for target practice; there were massive bleeding ulcers spread everywhere, and even Rembrandt said it was one of the sickest colons he had ever seen.

The revised diagnosis didn't change much, but it further convinced us we had made a good choice by coming to Mayo. The unparalleled acumen of Rembrandt and his cohorts gave us the freedom to rest and heal, as opposed to constantly having to serve as our own advocate, which we had done in many other hospitals. The seamless interdepartmental communication at Mayo ensured that every nurse or doctor that walked into Kailen's room knew her case intimately. As Jeff put it, they were a well-oiled machine.

The post-surgical hospital stay lasted five days. During that time, the nausea got significantly worse, Kailen developed a severe case of thrush which led to the development of open sores on her tongue and throat, and her gratuitous need for IV fluids led to massive swelling in her legs, hips, and abdomen.

To add insult to injury, she had also accidentally touched the anti-nausea patch behind her ear. Which normally wouldn't be a big deal, except she scratched her eye with the same hand. This caused dramatic mydriasis, or pupillary dilation, which essentially blinded her for the next forty-eight hours.

She was discharged on March 21st and I pushed her out of the hospital in a wheelchair. We spent the next several days at the hotel, taking intermittent trips back to the Clinic for checkups. Things were better but not by much. The swelling was debilitating, as was the nausea, and eating solid food was almost unthinkable. She didn't have any weight left to lose, and yet she was still losing it.

I remember carrying her to the bathroom. She desperately wanted to take a bath, to soak in the warm water, but she couldn't due to risk of infecting the incision site. So, I turned on the shower and let it cascade over her emaciated body. And though she was facing away from me, I could hear the guttural sobs coming from her chest.

She was in enormous pain, so swollen and sore she

could barely move. When I lifted her out of the tub, it was like lifting a skeleton; her body was shrunken, reduced down to nothing more than bone and sinew. She was bald and pale and disintegrating right before my eyes.

But I didn't cry. Not in front of her.

I maintained my equanimity.

Rembrandt cleared Kailen to get on an airplane on March 24th. I flew home that morning so I could get back in time for class, while she and her parents departed Rochester's farmhouse airport late that afternoon.

Unfortunately, though Kailen had already endured what most would consider a lifetime's worth of hardship, she was about to embark upon the most hellish month of her life.

And this is part of the story only she can tell.

♥ ♥ ♥

TeamKCT blog post (April 4th, 2013):

> *Good day, everyone! And I do not say that lightly. A few days ago I would not have been able to put the words "good" and "day" in the same sentence. But praise God, I am now in a much better place.*
>
> *The past 2 weeks since I left Mayo have truly felt like a trip through hell and back and I have*

had neither the time nor energy to update anyone. So, I will start this post where we left off and walk you through all that has happened as best I can. Prepare yourself for one wild ride!

Last you heard from me I had just been discharged from the hospital in Rochester and was headed back to the hotel for a few days of healing before flying back home. When I left the hospital, I was happy to be in a regular bed and to walk around more than just the hospital hallways, but the healing process ended up not going as smoothly as I had hoped it would. It seemed that every rare and unusual complication that could happen was happening, and it was making things extremely difficult.

First, I received a lot if IV fluids after surgery, which is normal, but when you've had two blood clots and the valves in your legs are broken, receiving a lot of fluid while lying in a hospital bed all day means the fluid pools up all over your body and doesn't get processed.

When I left the hospital at Mayo, I had 13 pounds of extra fluid in my legs, hips, and abdomen that made it impossible to walk, much less wear pants! Other than the baggiest pair of Bryan's old sweatpants I could find to lounge around in. I wore those for days because nothing else would fit! Then all through the days following discharge, mom, dad, and Bryan would take turns rubbing my legs, trying to squeeze the fluid like toothpaste out of a tube.

Even if you don't.

Second, I developed a nasty case of thrush in my mouth which made it impossible to eat or drink. Thrush is an infection that causes your mouth and tongue to be coated in all this nasty white stuff with bumps all over. It burns and bleeds and all I could do was keep swishing my mouth with this medicine that would numb it long enough to let me take a few bites of food.

Third, I was having trouble seeing because I somehow touched the nausea patch I had after surgery and then touched my eyes...So, basically, I was a pudgy, fluid-filled, burnt-mouthed, puking, blind, sore all over, unable to walk, aching, weak, mess of a girl for a few days...

The Rochester airport was amazingly understanding and didn't even make me get out of my wheelchair to go through security! They took me to a private room with a hospital bed where I could lay and prop my feet up until our plane arrived.

We waited about an hour and then boarded the plane first so I could get situated. Thank God no one sat next to me, so I was able to put my feet up in the seat beside me...I was feeling ok when we first boarded, but as soon as we took off, boom hits the nausea. I ended up throwing up all through take-off and landing and felt like I was going to explode with all the fluid build-up and changes in pressure...The worst part was I couldn't even enjoy the fact that I didn't have to worry about going to the bathroom during the flight.

We made our connecting flight in Minneapolis and once again, since dad had called ahead, the airport took really good care of me. A skycab was waiting at the gate and drove us across the entire airport.

The ride felt like 20 minutes even though it was probably more like 7, but when your back feels like someone is stabbing you all over, you can barely hold yourself up because of sutures in your abdomen, you have puked 5 times in the last hour, you have 13 pounds of fluid trying to pool in your ankles, and you know you have a whole second flight ahead of you, time doesn't exactly pass quickly. And it didn't help that the whole airport was staring at "the girl with cancer, riding on a cart, and wearing whatever clothes she could actually fit around her swollen body." It seemed I had a spotlight above me and every person was watching as I rode by.

At that point, I was literally praying God would just let me pass out and wake up at my parents' house. I didn't feel as though I could take another step.

But God had mercy on my body and I made it on to the next plane. I still threw up taking off and landing on the second flight, but the fact that we were landing in Louisville helped me hold on and finish out the journey.

We got off the plane, I got in my wheelchair,

Even if you don't.

and we managed to get all our luggage without complication. Praise God. My aunt picked us up and as we drove home, I could not have been more relieved to see my parents' house.

I shuffled inside, dad carried me up the stairs, and I went right to bed. I was home, finally, and holding on to the fact that I was only going to get better from here...

But I was SO wrong.

TeamKCT blog post (April 8th, 2013):

All righty, so we move to part II of the journey through hell and back. And unfortunately, the worst is still yet to come.

We left off with me on my memory foam mattress, propped up on an abundance of pillows, with my feet elevated to allow all the fluid to drain out of my legs. I set up the plethora of pills I was taking around the clock to manage pain and fight nausea, and we all went to bed thinking I was finally beginning the healing process.

I slept fitfully that night, but still rested more than I had since surgery. I was still fighting nausea pretty badly and having to take pills all night on an empty stomach wasn't helping...Not to mention, I don't remember the last time I slept through the night anyway. Seriously. I know as a kid I used to sleep and wake up feeling refreshed and like the night flew by because I slept all the way through, but I haven't slept for a whole night in at least a decade, if not longer.

I started out going to the bathroom only once or twice a night in middle school, but just before surgery, it wasn't unusual for me to wake every hour of the night to use the restroom. I had gotten used to that routine and now my body doesn't even know how to sleep anymore. I keep waking up and feeling like I'm forgetting something. But despite all that, I did get a little rest that first night home.

The next day, I decided to stay in bed and let my body do whatever it needed. I would take my meds and make sure I drank enough but I wasn't going to force anything...I stayed hydrated, ate a few cheerios every now and then, and napped as needed.

I did, however, need to go see my oncologist. Since we had been away at Mayo, I was late for my monthly hormone suppressant shot for the breast cancer. I knew I needed to continue treatment ASAP, so I mustered all my strength, put Bryan's lifesaving baggy sweatpants back on, and off mom and I went to the doctor.

I was doing alright until a little way into the drive when I suddenly began to ache all over and have a horrible pain in my lower back. We made it to the office and I was immediately taken back and put into a bed where I could lay and take the pressure off my abdomen. I felt better at first, but the pain in my back started getting stronger and stronger.

My doctor came in and we caught up on Mayo and discussed how cancer treatment would eventually resume. By the end of the talk, I could barely speak my back was hurting so bad. We figured it was just pain from surgery and flying and everything, but I ended up needing morphine before we left and still had to get a huge intramuscular shot in my abdomen just above my fresh incisions and ileostomy. Talk about ouch!

But I made it through and was taken out to the car in a wheelchair. Once again, I survived the car ride home only by the grace of God and holding on to the fact that I was going back to my comfy bed. And thank goodness, I had nowhere to go the next day so NOW I could really and truly, FINALLY, rest and heal for real.

And, once again, I could not have been more wrong.

I tried to eat before going to bed that night, and after a few bites, the vomiting began in all its glory. I threw up into the night and ended up "sleeping" sitting up. It made for a long night, but the next day is when the worst set in.

I won't bore you with all the details, but

119

basically, for the next two days, I felt like acid was always about to come up my throat, I could throw up on command, I couldn't walk, I couldn't eat, I couldn't drink, and I was beyond miserable. I couldn't lay down, but I couldn't sit up. If I moved too much, acid would bubble all in my belly, but if I didn't move enough I would get even more sore and achy all over. I didn't leave my room for two days and my spirit was sinking lower by the minute.

I can truly say those few days were the darkest days of my life. I know the difference between happiness and joy, and while I know I'm not always happy, I always feel God's joy with me. The Joy of the Lord is my strength. That's how I survive all I go through (that's my secret).

But in those days, I wasn't sure I could feel God with me anymore. And that scared me. This surgery was supposed to be my freedom. It was supposed to be my last step. After this surgery, I was supposed to be free and unchained from the bathroom. I was supposed to have my life back. So, why was I stuck in bed, literally unable to do anything but breathe? I didn't get it and I didn't understand why it was happening. After years and years, I had finally come to accept that this surgery was a good thing, and yet I felt worse than I ever had before.

WHAT. WAS. GOING. ON?!

Then, by late afternoon on Wednesday, my

Even if you don't.

stoma stopped having output. So, no eating, no drinking, lots of puking, and no output. Things had gotten serious and I knew in my heart they weren't going to get better. I packed my bags for the ER, the last place on earth I wanted to go, and back to the hospital we went.

By now I was so exhausted and sick of being sick I didn't know how I was going to survive another stay in the hospital. I had just gotten out of one! I basically went on autopilot and decided to survive moment-by-moment. Surely I would turn a corner soon. SURELY. That's all I had to hold on to.

Mom, dad, and I waited a few minutes before being taken back to the ER at Baptist, but not before having two nurses say something about remembering me. You know you've had some rough times when you're only 23 and the ER nurses recognize you when you walk in!

I got into bed and mindlessly went through the whole routine of medical history, symptoms, list of current medications, and the rest of the registration process. Then the nurse came in to access my port so they could draw blood and get fluids started since I was dehydrated again.

I normally talk with all my nurses, smile, joke, and am always happy. I always try to look at my situation as an opportunity to show God to others in spite of all I'm going through. I always show my joy. But that day, I had nothing left in me to show.

When I realized that, I knew there was something badly wrong. But, as God always does, He showed up when I needed Him most.

Turns out my nurse was a cancer survivor, and as he worked on my labs and spoke encouragement to me, I could feel a small spark of joy come back into my heart. Praise God, for His timing is perfect.

After the nurse left, the doctor came in to examine me. He checked my abdomen and pressed around a little. He asked if I felt any pain where he was pushing on my left side and I said no. I mean, I had just had surgery and had fresh incisions and all, so yeah, I was sore. But I didn't feel anything beyond what I thought would be normal.

Nonetheless, he went ahead and ordered morphine and some nausea meds. Both were injected into my port and as soon as the morphine hit and I felt relief from what I had been feeling the past 3 days, I realized just how much pain I was truly in.

After the doctor examined me, he ordered a CT scan to look at my abdomen. We waited a while, eventually got a private room, and I was finally taken back for the scan. Having done a million MRIs with all the cancer stuff, I was very happy to see the CT machine (although feeling like you've peed yourself whenever they inject the contrast is not the most pleasant of feelings!).

Even if you don't.

Anyway, a few minutes in the machine, quite a few more minutes waiting for the results, and then the doctor finally came back in with the news.

Turns out I had a massive abscess of fluid in the left side of my abdomen. The big question was why.

Either I had an infection that had just somehow gotten in there while I was opened up, or worst-case scenario, I had a leak in my small intestine that was causing fluid build-up. If the second were true, that meant they would have to go back in for another surgery. So, of course, we immediately started praying it was an infection that could be drained and treated with antibiotics.

I couldn't keep anything down because my stomach was being compressed to half its normal size by the pocket of fluid. Not to mention, the massive abscess was also pinching nerves in my back – thus the back pain – and pushing on all my organs that were already sensitive from having just shifted to fill the void where my colon was.

ARE YOU KIDDING ME?! REALLY??

I just wanted to laugh and cry and completely spaz out! It seemed that just when I thought things were going to be better, the exact opposite would happen. Whatever rare, unusual complication that could happen, was, without fail, going to happen. And while I know that isn't true, in the moment when you are weak and tired, it's very hard to see beyond the pain.

Upon waiting a while longer, we learned there was no one at Baptist who was comfortable handling my case. I was going to be transferred downtown to University, which had a more experienced colorectal team.

After being loaded up on one bumpy, painful, late night, ambulance ride into downtown Louisville, I settled into my first room at University and learned that I would have to wait until morning before they could place a drain tube.

Bryan was now on his way from Lexington since we knew this was going to be more than a quick visit to the ER and suddenly, once again, we all found ourselves in an all too familiar scenario...

TeamKCT blog post (April 12th, 2013):

It was about midnight at this point, and even though I was on pain meds, I was still brilliant enough to reach the agonizing conclusion that I was going to have to wait the entire night before I would be seen by anyone. As you might have guessed, I was thrilled by this realization and it did wonders for my morale...not.

Even if you don't.

I did, however, feel a little better once a nurse came in and told us we would be getting a newer, bigger room. Of course, "shortly" meant 3 hours later, but by that time Bryan had arrived and I was much better off, considering I hadn't seen him since we said goodbye at the hotel in Rochester.

(Side note: Bryan and I have been married for a bit over 2 years now, but I still get butterflies when he walks into the room. And, for some reason, when we have been apart for a while and are reunited, I'm still amazed when I feel him hold me up. No, not literally hold me up, but that moment when I start to breathe easier, my shoulders relax, and I'm able to rest in him knowing he is one with me. He often knows what I need just by looking into my eyes, and there is a peace I feel because I know I am safe with him.

That might all just sound mushy gushy to you, but it's huge for me. For years and years, as I walked through my health stuff, my parents were the only ones who had any idea what I battled on a daily basis. Not even my closest friends knew because I didn't tell anyone.

It was easier to handle things if I did it myself because, well, I knew I could always count on me. And because of the nature of what I dealt with, I didn't even let my mom help me carry things as much as I should have.

I didn't know any of that until Bryan and I

got married and we began to feel a distance between us. I was still taking care of me and didn't need anyone else; when Bryan tried to help, I felt vulnerable and pushed him away for a long time. And boy, did I not know what I was missing out on!

When I finally learned how to share my burdens with Bryan, my life became infinitely better. I thought I had perfected my ways and had become as efficient at dealing with my stuff as possible, but enter Bryan, and suddenly my burden was only half as heavy and I wished I had let him support me much sooner...Anyway, I was happy to see my husband. Back to the story...)

Now it's 3:00 AM, we just got to my new room, which was considerably bigger with a couch and chairs, and it was time to settle in for a few hours until the doctors made their rounds in the early morning. We were told that a doctor from the colorectal team would come see me and tell us when I would be getting a drain tube placed in my side.

We tried to get a couple hours' rest before the big day began.

One minor, yet extremely inconvenient detail: I hadn't had anything to eat or drink in over 12 hours, and the only thing allowed to sate my pallet was a gross, minty sponge on a stick that I could dip in water...

Even if you don't.

Around 8:00 the next morning, one of the doctors from the colorectal team came by and told us I would be going shortly to have the drain placed. Transport came and took me downstairs where I talked with the doctor who would be placing the drain and answered a few standard questions. He was sweet and kept trying to reassure me it wouldn't hurt too bad and I probably wouldn't even remember it because of the medicine.

In my head I was laughing, thinking, "If this guy knew all I've been through, he wouldn't even bother trying to comfort me." So I looked at him, smiled and said, "I've had ribs pop out, a bone biopsy, and survived chemotherapy. If you could just get me one of those sponge-on-a-stick things, I think I'll be okay."

Luckily, after I got my sponge-on-a-stick, I was very painfully moved onto the CT table and given Versed, so my lack of verbal filter didn't matter as much. The last thing I remember is the nurse asking me to raise my left arm above my head. After that, I woke up in the hallway...

Once back in the room, they set me up on a morphine pump, and when it eventually caught up with the pain, I had a rather uneventful day and got a small bit of sleep.

The next day, Friday, was day 3 in the hospital. There are many things I could say about this day – bizarre interactions with our nurse (who we now refer to as Cowboy Tom), lack of communication from any doctor, learning how to function in the one hospital in Louisville I've never been in, and a whole lot more.

I won't go on and on with details, but our experience was pretty awful and it was quickly going further downhill. At least I felt alright that day compared to how I had been feeling. And when they checked the bag connected to my side, we found out I was feeling better because they had drained 2 liters (and counting) of infectious fluid from the abscess!

Now I'm not saying I'm the world's smallest woman, but I'm not a very big person. And to think I had 2 liters of anything in my stomach was a bit disconcerting! I was just glad it was gone and now I could get better...

Yup, you guessed it. Once again, I could not have EVER been more wrong.

Day 3 ended and as Bryan and I settled in for the night, I was feeling pretty good about where I was. I wasn't on the morphine pump anymore, I was keeping food and medicine down, I was walking to the bathroom a little easier, and now all I had to do was hold on until Monday when I was projected to be discharged.

I didn't get much sleep that night, but I finally slept pretty hard from 5:00 AM to 6:30. I woke up just before my night nurse came in to introduce me to the day nurse who would be

Even if you don't.

taking over at 7:00. They left the room, and as I laid there in bed and my mind and body began to wake up, there was suddenly another feeling that was waking up, too.

Pain.

Bryan was asleep on the couch, desperately holding on to the last hours of "night," but I knew I had to wake him up. Things were about to get ugly.

As the pain intensified, I managed to say Bryan's name loud enough to wake him, and with one look at my face, he knew something was wrong. We called for the nurse, and when he came in, he asked about my pain level. To give some reference points: after colon removal at Mayo, I was at about a 3. The plane ride home from Mayo was a 4. The bone biopsy was a 6. And the worst pain I had ever felt in my life before this whole saga, when my rib popped out of place the first time, that was a 7.

When my nurse asked what my pain was at that moment, I was an 8. A solid 8.

I felt like a sword was being pushed in and out of my side where the tube was. I felt like someone had brutally beaten my left rib cage with a baseball bat. My lower back was one massive, throbbing knot of muscle, as was my left shoulder. My entire abdomen felt like I had just finished the most intense ab workout ever. My lower abs cringed with any movement. And every shallow breath I could manage sent searing pains stabbing and pulsing through my entire body.

I have never in my life been in so much pain and felt so weak and helpless.

Praise God for my nurse that day. He was truly an angel for us. He set right to getting me the pain medicine I needed and I could actually rest. He brought in a pain pill, but I couldn't even lift it to my mouth without causing debilitating pain. He stayed and helped me get it down, then asked how many days post-surgery I was. Bryan told him this was day 3 after surgery and the nurse was quiet for a second. He asked if I'd had a morphine pump, and if so, why I didn't have one now seeing as days 2-3 are the worst after drain tube placement...

ARE. YOU. KIDDING. ME?!

I don't know how we weren't told and I was in too much pain to even think about it. All I wanted was for someone to knock me out and wake me up on Monday.

My nurse went to get morphine, and while he was gone, tears began flowing from my eyes. Not the tears like, "this really hurts so I need to cry," and not even the "I am so frustrated right now I don't even have words" kind of tears, though I was feeling both of those things. These tears were involuntary and seemed to be streaming directly from the pain itself. I

Even if you don't.

couldn't help it, so I just laid there and cried.

Bryan held my hand and cried out to God for me, but I'll admit, at that point I didn't really feel like talking to God. I was more in a place of "God, I think it's pretty obvious what the desire of my heart is right now so please hear me. If not, then I'll have to talk to you later."

I know that wasn't the most mature or spiritual response, but I'm just being honest and that's exactly where my flesh was at that point. In fact, if God had asked me right then and there if I was okay to go ahead and leave this world, I probably would have thrown in the towel and asked Him to take me home.

We spent the rest of that day getting morphine every 2 hours and pain pills every 4, but it wasn't until after dinner that the medicine finally caught up to the pain. Even though I was feeling better, I didn't sleep at all that night. I was too afraid of waking up like I had that morning, so I figured I would just stay awake and try to move around enough to stay loose.

By morning, my plan had worked and I wasn't sore. I was just tired.

Over the next couple of days, Mom and Bryan took turns staying with me and we had a good time amongst ourselves. We have developed a pretty functional way of living in a hospital and we all flow well together. We make each other laugh a lot and have a saying: "If *you don't make your own fun, you won't have any fun." And in our lives right now, that's pretty much true.*

I stayed on a lot of pain medicines and seemed to be doing ok. I didn't get any worse and felt like I was at least making a little progress. I could sometimes lift my leg halfway up the bed without having to have someone do it for me and that was big progress! My poor muscles had atrophied so badly I couldn't have done a squat to save my life.

Chicken legs were happening major...and who am I kidding, they still are, ok!

The best part over the next two days was that I had visitors. It was medicine for my spirit to be with family, and while they were there I could feel my joy growing back. My favorite part was when my Uncle Steve and Uncle Donnie knelt on either side of my bed and prayed over me as my aunts, parents, siblings, and Bryan joined in around the room.

You may have never experienced this, but for me there is just something about when men of God pray over me that seems to breathe the very life of the Almighty into the core of my being. It speaks to my soul and makes my spirit rise up like nothing else in this world...It does my soul good when men of God rise up, boldly take their place as sons of the King, and claim what is rightfully theirs over those they look after.

Even if you don't.

Then came Sunday, day 5, and the day of the resurrection of our Savior Jesus Christ. I wasn't getting up and putting on my Easter dress; I was in a hospital gown in a bed. I wasn't going to hunt Easter eggs with my cousins; I was barely able to walk to the bathroom. But I was humbled, knowing how miserable I had been the last few weeks, when I thought about how it compared to the sacrifice Jesus made on the cross.

I wasn't able to go to church that Resurrection Day, but it was the most real Easter I had ever experienced.

Bryan left that night to go back to Lexington and class the next day and we all prayed I would be able to go home as planned. Monday morning, I went in for a drain study where they checked on the abscess. They did the study, and a few hours later I was given my freedom!

Mom and dad packed up my things, I got myself cleaned up, and yup, once again, I donned Bryan's infamous baseball sweatpants! I plopped my swollen body down in that wheelchair and I was outta there!

After we made it to my parents' house, I was already worn out, but I had enough energy left to pack my things and make the ride back to Lexington. This would be my first time home in almost a month, my first time seeing Layla in several weeks, and my first time to ever be in my own home and not be chained to a bathroom.

I knew there were still trials ahead, but I could finally see the light. God had not failed me. I had not given up. My parents and Bryan had survived with me. We had all been through hell and back, and now it was time to heal.

Finally, the worst truly was over and only better was yet to come.

Praise God. He is good.

Unfortunately, Kailen was only partly right.

God *is* good, but the worst was far from over.

One of my favorite movie moments is the final scene from *Gladiator*, when Maximus walks slowly through a field of wheat to be reunited with his family.

In the scene, the field serves as an idyllic pathway from one life to the next, the golden grain swaying gently beneath his fingertips, beckoning him forward. It's powerful cinematography, but the scene's true resonance is generated by the music.

The song is entitled, *"Now We Are Free,"* by Hans Zimmer and Lisa Gerrard. I'm not a musician, and I'm certainly no musical critic, but Zimmer and Gerrard seem to perfectly capture what it would feel like to undo the bindings of this world and move on to something greater.

Though Maximus has just been killed by a vile dictator, the song helps us understand that death can be a mercy. We see that come to fruition when Maximus's young son runs and jumps into his arms: unjustly separated in life, redemptively united in death.

When Kailen finally came home, having endured a month-long nightmare, we tried our best to re-establish normality. I went to class, helped her make meals, we became irrevocably addicted to the show *Friends*, we read together, prayed together, and tried to stay faithful to the hope of healing. But unfortunately, she was just too uncomfortable for anything to feel normal.

The abdominal drain was cumbersome and painful – a long, narrow tube that snaked out of her side and emptied purulent pink fluid into a bag – and she was still battling nausea. We tried to celebrate the victory that she was no longer chained to the bathroom, but it's tough to celebrate when every movement hurts and you're tasting every meal twice.

Kailen spent large swaths of the day confined to bed. She read and wrote and quite literally taught herself how to knit and crochet, always making the best of the situation, but there was no hiding her misery. It seemed we had merely traded one bondage for another, a sick colon for an ileostomy bag and a sadistic drain tube.

And, of course, there was the small matter of the terminal cancer insidiously consuming her breast and bones.

Before starting chemo, Kailen's friends had bought her a pair of purple Beats headphones. They looked almost cartoonish on her little head, but she loved them. Admittedly, I used them, too. Their sound quality was amazing, but my favorite feature was actually their sound-cancelling ability. I would sometimes wear them while I studied just to relish the sound of complete and total silence.

One night, I got out of the shower and found her lying in bed, in the only position that gave her any relief, mummified with blankets as always.

But there was one key difference: her hands were raised high toward the ceiling.

I asked if everything was okay, twice, and she didn't answer. Worried, I hurried over to the bed and realized she had on the Beats, the huge purple headphones enveloping her ears, and her eyes were closed. She couldn't see or hear me; she was lost in worship.

My towel had fallen off, but I just stood there and watched her, transfixed by her unshakable faith. I eventually grabbed my phone and took a picture of her. About that time, she opened her eyes and looked at me with this strange knowing expression, like she had been told a secret. She took off the headphones and handed them to me.

"Listen to this," she said. "Just close your eyes and listen."

I laid on the bed beside her, still dripping wet from the shower, and put on the Beats. The music was loud and almost instantly consumed me. My head fell against the pillow and I closed my eyes as the haunting notes washed over me, as the scene played in my mind: *the wheat field, gold and swaying.*

While "Now We Are Free" boomed into my ears, I thought of what Kailen had seen, of the secret she knew, and I wanted to cry because now I knew it, too.

We eventually fell asleep like that, and a few hours later I woke up to Kailen packing her bags.

"What's wrong?" I asked.

She had been crying. "It's back," she said, pointing to her stomach. "The abscess is back."

After being home just thirteen days, we were about to start the battle all over again.

That early morning drive to Louisville was the first time I ever shouted at God. It also marked the beginning of a season in which Kailen and I lived our life in two-week increments.

Neither of us had slept a full night in over a month, so we pulled into the parking structure at University Hospital in a mental, emotional, and literal fog. As we walked across the catwalk into the hospital, a pernicious mixture of déjà vu and post-traumatic stress took hold. All we could do was take the next step and pray that maybe this was the visit that would finally put us on the road to healing.

We were VIP by this point and were fast-tracked

past registration back into our old room. A doctor from the colorectal team saw us a few hours later and took Kailen for yet another abdominal CT scan.

The results were bad: she had two newly-formed abscesses that were loculated, a fancy medical term meaning separated or walled-off, from the main abscess cavity. The possible causes were many, but none posed positive eventualities.

We spent yet another fitful night at University and were greeted early the next morning with the revelatory news that the drain wasn't working properly. According to the surgeon, who was a poor excuse for a Rembrandt, and frankly one of the rudest, most arrogant people I've ever met, the problem was likely three-fold: 1) The drain wasn't large enough to accommodate the fluid volume, and 2) It was positioned too high in the abdomen to reach the loculated portions of the abscess, and 3) It was probably clogged and causing backflow.

Dr. Not-Rembrandt scheduled another drain procedure for that evening. The plan was to go back in and either place a larger drain, reposition the current drain, or possibly add a new drain.

Basically, when it came to drains, they had no idea what they were doing.

Which is why, when further imaging revealed the small hole in Kailen's rectal stump that had caused the whole mess, we called Mayo. And after sending them the records from our stay at University, the Mayo gastroenterologist recommended we fly back to Rochester and let him and his team reposition the drain.

While we weren't exactly thrilled with the news, we were confident that if anyone could make this better, it was the team at Mayo.

Kailen and Kim flew back to Rochester the next week, but not before two very important milestones were reached.

First, we became a family of four.

As I've stated previously, Kailen maintained very specific prayer requests. One of those requests had always been a large, male, reverse-brindle boxer puppy. So, even though he arrived a few months late for her 23rd birthday, I bought her our second child and first boy, Rupp.

Though Kailen loved Rupp more than just about anything in the world, the second milestone was far more significant. The news came on the morning of April 23rd. It was the day of the flight, but Kailen had seen Dr. Williams that morning for a quick check-up.

I was riding my bike to class when I got the call.

Remission. The cancer was in remission.

Suddenly the spring air felt new and reviving, and as I breathed it in, pedaling ever-faster in my state of euphoria, I once again felt an overwhelming sense of God's omnipotence.

I temporarily forgot about the seven months of hell we had just endured, about the dire prognosis we were staring down. Because on that cool April morning, for a single fleeting moment, it seemed everything was going to be okay.

♥ ♥ ♥

The trip to Mayo was brief and fruitful.

Kailen had two appointments, one with an interventional radiologist, who placed a new drain lower in Kailen's abdomen, and another with her gastroenterologist. He confirmed that the main abscess cavity was nearly empty and healing nicely, but the two smaller abscesses were secondary to the leak in the rectal stump. It was problematic and potentially serious, he explained, but not altogether unexpected considering the severity of the Crohn's.

Two weeks. They would re-check the drain in two weeks with the hope of removing it. Until then, all we could do was wait and let Kailen's body heal. So Kim and Kailen enjoyed Rochester that evening, then flew back home the next day.

They made it back in time for Jarrod's spring football game at Georgetown College, where Kailen was called onto the field and honored at halftime. I was in between the spring semester and my summer internship, so we cherished some much-needed downtime together. We spent long, lazy days at home, walking Layla and incessantly admonishing Rupp for pooping in the floor.

A week later, Kailen spoke to a youth group about how to remain joyous in suffering.

Even if you don't.

She wrote this about the experience (taken from TeamKCT blog post, May 3rd, 2013):

The main reason I was so happy for last night's opportunity was because, after the initial shock of the cancer diagnosis wore off, I began looking forward to sharing all that God has done, and is doing, in my life.

At times, that was the only thing keeping me going: knowing that God was going to use all the suffering for good even when the devil intended it all for bad...

Speaking to those kids last night, as well as these blog entries, are just the first of many punches I intend to throw back at the king of lies after he has tried so hard to take me out of the fight. I got news for ya buddy, ain't gonna happen!

I will fight with all I have and tell as many people as I can about the goodness and power of the Almighty God!

A few days later, we flew back to Mayo. Kailen and I ate dinner at an authentic Irish pub called McGoon's, then sipped coffee and bought some books at our Barnes and Noble. We were making Rochester a vacation destination because we really didn't have a choice. After all, if we didn't make our own fun, we weren't going to have any.

The next day's appointment wasn't what we were hoping for: two more weeks. The cavity was healing wonderfully and there were only two milliliters of fluid left in the abscess, but it was still too early to remove the drain. So, again, we flew home with plans of flying right back two weeks later.

The following weekend, Kailen's grandmother, aka Mae-ma, organized another Team KCT benefit. This time it was in Monticello, a small town in eastern Kentucky, and the turnout was massive.

People that barely knew Kailen auctioned items and gave money to help us continue our fight. She spoke again that day, and I remember watching from the bleachers, wondering why God had chosen a schmuck like me to fight alongside such an exceptional human being.

I had already started my internship when it came time for the next trip, so Jeff accompanied Kailen to Rochester. It was another short trip with unfortunate results; despite the cavity being in excellent condition and completely empty, there was still a canal linking the abscess cavity to the rectal stump. As long as the canal persisted, the potential for recurrent infection remained high. They conducted an outpatient procedure where they "shot" the rectal stump with metal clamps, trying to once-and-for-all seal the leak. But for now, the drain stayed.

Another two weeks.

Meanwhile, news on the cancer side of things remained positive. Kailen's iron levels were higher than they had ever been – a result of eliminating the copious rectal bleeding – tumor markers were down, and the tumor itself had shrunk considerably. Dr. Williams told us the remission was holding, but he scheduled a PET scan and MRIs a few weeks later to confirm.

Life was still tough, and managing a flight to Minnesota every two weeks was quickly growing trite (and expensive), but we were grateful for all the healing God had accomplished.

We were learning that life is all about perspective.

TeamKCT blog post (May 31st, 2013):

> *9 months ago, I couldn't sleep, I couldn't exercise, I ate the same things all the time, I couldn't drink coffee, I couldn't ride in a car, and I couldn't even go get my own groceries. But today, I sleep better than I have in years, I work out every day, I eat anything I want, I drank 3 cups of coffee this morning, I can go on a road trip anywhere, and I not only go get my own groceries, but I can even carry them up the stairs by myself!*

> *I know those things aren't necessarily miraculous, but when I couldn't do any of them before, much less all in one day, every single one of them feels like a miracle to me.*

> *I have a life again. I am living again.*

Our next trip to Mayo was in early-June. When the gastro first told us the drain still couldn't come out, we were beginning to wonder if this was some type of cruel joke with no punch line, like living inside an M.C.

Escher lithograph.

But there was one small catch, he told us. The canal had not fully sealed, and though the metal clamps were in place, the rectal tissue was still so weakened from the Crohn's that it hadn't re-formed around the clamps. Thus, the rectal leak and the canal linking it to the abscess cavity still put Kailen at serious risk for recurrence and possible sepsis.

So, turns out, the need for a drain was indefinite. But there *was* a catch, one small ray of light in which to take heart: the external drain could be removed and replaced with a smaller, less obtrusive internal drain. It wasn't exactly what we had been praying for, but the thought of finally getting the tube out of her side and not having to lug a bag full of tomato-soup-looking fluid around sure sounded like an answered prayer.

They performed the procedure the next day with no complications. And after undergoing the PET scan and MRIs Dr. Williams had ordered, another round of appointments was complete.

We flew back home on Friday, but not before experiencing one of Rochester's most popular summer events: *Thursday on First.*

TOF runs weekly from the beginning of June through the end of August and assembles food trucks and local vendors along first street and Peace Plaza downtown. Thousands gather to eat and peruse the various tent displays, and considering Mayo Rochester is one of the premier hospitals in the world, people-watching became my and Kailen's favorite TOF pastime. We watched as folks from all over the world strolled through the Plaza and formulated grandiose narratives about where they were from and why they were here, all the while wondering if someone was doing the same to us.

The morning before our flight we established our official Rochester breakfast dive: Pannekoeken. It was a hole-in-the-wall beneath a hotel that served these Dutch, fluffy, oven-baked pancakes – *Pannekoeken* means *pancake* in Dutch – and you could get them stuffed with just about anything, from bananas and rum sauce, to strawberries, to chocolate chips, to bacon.

The place was painted green and pale orange, which made it look like you were eating inside a cantaloupe. And as Kailen so artfully put it, "Who wouldn't be happy eating inside a melon?"

We certainly were.

Later that day, we held hands during the cab ride to the airport and breathed a collective sigh of relief. It had been a productive trip, and it seemed we were finally where we wanted to be: Crohn's-free, drain-free, and cancer in remission.

But, as always, our relief was short-lived.

I stepped onto the balcony and looked out across the Atlantic, the water brackish and unending.

The ocean breeze was cool just after daybreak and it

tousled my hair as I leaned against the railing. Kailen was still asleep, so I sipped coffee and read my devotional in silence.

It was mid-August and we were in Hilton Head, our first vacation since our honeymoon. I watched the waves pound incessantly against the shoreline, the tide slowly receding, and reflected on the last two months. It had been a long summer.

Six days after we returned from Mayo, we received some excellent news: the PET scan looked great. The primary and metastatic sites were still lighting up on the scans, but they were dim, a faint glimmer of their former selves. The chemo had worked and the hormone suppressants were maintaining the fight. We had an appointment with Dr. Williams at the end of June, at which we expected to hear nothing but a more detailed analysis of the good news.

The first sign of trouble arrived on June 20th. And this time it had nothing to do with Kailen.

I was in Birmingham working my annual fireworks gig when Kailen called and told me her mom was in the hospital. Kim had been diagnosed with a blood clotting disorder, similar to Kailen's, and they had found evidence of two strokes.

Needless to say, we were all shocked. The blood clotting disorder was purportedly genetic, and though it had likely caused the strokes, the sheer stress of having a daughter battling cancer could have also triggered the events. Thankfully, Kim was doing well. The strokes would have some minor long-term effects, but nothing devastating.

Still, it was a sobering reminder that war has consequences.

A few days later, I drove back from Birmingham for a friend's wedding. Kailen and I were at the rehearsal dinner, sitting at a breezy outdoor café in Frankfort, when she got a text from Dr. Williams. There was a questionable spot on one of the MRIs. He told us not to worry, that it was probably insignificant, but I felt panicky the rest of the evening.

The wedding was the next day. It was a nice ceremony, but really all I remember was an apocalyptically stupid comment made by the pastor. He was attempting to illustrate the hackneyed and much-beleaguered point that marriage is tough and you're going to have to band together during hard times. He made some joke that wasn't funny, then proceeded to ask the rhetorical question, "What are you going to do when money is tight and the dryer goes out?"

I wanted to stand up and say, "Shove your dryer where it don't fit, sir. When you're twenty-four and your wife has terminal cancer, then maybe you can come back and preach at me about the assorted hardships of life."

But I didn't. It wasn't his fault.

Kailen was standing on stage with the other bridesmaids, and one look at her told me she was thinking the same thing. Everyone else in the room was smiling, pleasantly oblivious, enamored by all the pretty colors and the existential splendor of the moment, while Kailen and I held one another's gaze, aliens lost in a world we had once known, surrounded by people that thought they knew us.

But they didn't.

And again, it wasn't really their fault.

Our appointment with Dr. Williams was on June 26th. Turns out the "little blip" on the MRI portended something far bigger; despite the clean PET scan, which had been performed just three weeks earlier, Kailen's tumor markers had almost doubled.

Dr. Williams tried to put us at ease, but he was realistic: this wasn't good news. He ordered a slew of repeat MRIs to try and locate the source of increased activity.

In the interlude, life went on. Kailen was feeling great and had joined something called Tone It Up (TIU). TIU is a diet and fitness lifestyle that bolsters its nutrition plans and daily workout regimens with a huge community of friends and encouragers. Kailen did her TIU workouts every single morning, we started running together, and we even joined a gym.

Despite the ominous news waiting on the horizon, the next few weeks were renewing for both body and mind. Our spirits were up and I had never seen Kailen in such great shape. The abolition of Crohn's had completely transformed her body, and with the ongoing support of the TIU community, her aspiration was to overcome every obstacle in her path and win the TIU

Even if you don't.

Bikini Series Grand Prize.

Unfortunately, the results from the most recent scans brought everything to an abrupt halt yet again. Cancerous activity had increased in her breast and bones, and though she had no new metastases, the tumor markers had doubled. *Again.*

We knew from the initial biopsies that the cancer was ER+ and PR+, meaning it was estrogen and progesterone receptor positive. This was the reason Kailen was put on hormone suppressants after chemotherapy. Dr. Williams explained that loss of adequate estrogen suppression was the likely culprit fueling the cancer's resurgence. Kailen was young, which made suppressing her estrogen difficult.

There was really only one foolproof way to do it, Williams told us, and it was very unpleasant.

He sent the scan results to Kailen's oncologist at Mayo, who then shared them with a breast surgeon. A tentative plan was constructed and it looked something like this:

1) Mastectomy ASAP

2) Immediately followed by radiation

3) If necessary, the unpleasant foolproof option: *ovary removal*

That's what I was thinking about as I watched the waves slam against the shore that morning in Hilton Head. We were in another moment of false reprieve, another mirage, another emotional island. I tried to enjoy the beauty and the solitude, but the weight of what was coming pressed in on me like the tide, making it hard to breathe.

We left that afternoon and drove back to Kentucky – back into the heat of battle, into surgery, and radiation, and another year of pharmacy school.

And as we drove, I silently wondered if that was the last time my sweet wife would ever see the ocean.

Three days before leaving for Mayo, Kailen ran in the Dirty Girl 5K, a mud run to benefit breast cancer research.

Several of her friends, including her sister, Kristen, and her best friend, Alex, ran alongside her. I didn't actually run in the race, but I might as well have. I jogged at least five kilometers along the outside of the course, taking pictures and yelling words of encouragement all the way to the finish line.

Kailen and her parents flew back to Rochester for a surgical consult on August 27th while I stayed behind and finished my first full week of classes. The consult was quick and the surgery was scheduled for August 30th.

By the time I joined her in Rochester the night before the procedure, Kailen could not have been more ready to get it over with.

Even if you don't.

TeamKCT blog post (August 26th, 2013):

> *The sooner I have surgery, the sooner I can live without this lump that just never quite seems to shut up. It has been very rude since it came to visit and one time it even tried to hurt me. But no matter, we will remove it gently and make sure it knows it is no longer welcome here.*

She was the most courageous person I have ever known. But she was human. So when they told her reconstruction wasn't possible, that it was too risky, that her prognosis didn't warrant such a risk, she felt it.

She felt the same hurt and disappointment anyone would feel upon hearing such news. But Kailen had a way of turning any negative into a positive, and that was a gift born directly from her faith in Jesus Christ.

TeamKCT blog post (August 30th, 2013):

> *I am definitely excited, a little sad, pumped to be closer to healing, yet already dreading being in pain and having to recover. But mostly, I am at peace. Ya'll must be praying up a storm because He is lavishing His peace on me!*

> *I know I am in good hands up here, I am coming out of surgery much healthier, and I will never again have to deal with the "ew, ew get it off me" feeling this lump gives me.*

> *Sometimes I feel like I am really going to miss having my very own breast (we've been sort of attached all these years), but then I*

151

remember that it tried to kill me and I'm ok with saying goodbye.

Kailen lived life like a fairytale, even though hers read more like a tragedy. She made jokes when none of us had any reason to laugh; she praised God when I wanted to cuss Him.

That is not to say she never cussed at God, or asked Him why He had allowed her youth to be stolen. There were moments, always in private, when her humanness shown through.

Even I have to remind myself sometimes – she was a person; she was real; she lived.

Believe it or not, the surgery went perfectly. The surgeon was able to achieve negative margins (meaning she got all the cancer), and she only had to remove one lymph node. The tumor was mobile and had not yet reached the skin, both of which were positive prognostic factors.

It had grown, though. Considerably. The tumor had doubled in diameter, from five centimeters to ten centimeters, since the end of chemo in February.

100% growth in just six months spoke to the cancer's aggressiveness. That wasn't good news for the metastatic sites.

Metastatic cancer kills because it can never be fully eradicated. By definition, it has left the primary site and spread throughout the body. This means that removal of the primary site, such as a breast in Kailen's case, is not curative; it is merely palliative – an effort to extend life, not save it. No matter how much chemotherapy or radiation Kailen's body endured, she would never be cured of cancer.

Medically speaking, as of September 13th, 2012, Kailen would never again be cancer free. Even if every cancer cell in her entire body was killed except for a sub-microscopic patch hidden somewhere in her bones, that patch would eventually grow, mutate, and metastasize somewhere else.

My professors taught me these things and the doctors frequently reminded us. Kailen understood it. In fact, she was smart enough that no one even had to tell her. She had a tangible grip on reality as of day one, but even still, her faith remained undeterred.

It was a paradox that defied earthly logic:

Kailen knew with full assurance God was going to heal her, and yet, at the same moment, understood she was dying.

Her faith was much stronger than mine; I *hoped* God would heal her, begged Him with all my heart, while realizing she was probably going to die. Kailen *knew* she was going to be healed and *knew* she was going to die.

I can't explain it, but it's the truth.

TeamKCT blog post (August 31st, 2013):

>   *The doctors may not say it, but I can and I*

will...I AM CANCER FREE!!! In the name of Jesus, I am cancer free.

♥ ♥ ♥

Summer was restoration and autumn was deconstruction.

In 2011, we had an idyllic summer followed by the start of pharmacy school and a cataclysmic argument that ended with me going on a manhunt. In 2012, we basked in summer's ethereal Americana, dreamed big dreams, ate popsicles, and watched the Olympics before receiving a terminal cancer diagnosis in September. 2014 and 2015 would go on to be even worse.

It was an unfailing pattern in our marriage; the sole exception was 2013.

There were no post-surgical complications. Yes, you heard me correctly: NONE. After the month-long debacle following Kailen's total colectomy, we were braced for the worst. But this time around, God answered our prayers. The mastectomy was a therapeutic success and we were cleared to fly home just four days after the procedure. No nausea, no edema, and no three-liter intraabdominal abscesses.

Further, Kailen saw a hematologist before leaving Mayo and he declared her medically healed of all blood clotting disorders. From a scientific standpoint, the test was either a false negative or the severity of the Crohn's disease had caused a false positive when Kailen was first diagnosed in high school. But from a faith standpoint, it was divine deliverance. God had performed yet another miracle in Kailen's body. And as we flew home, we rested in the hope that if God could make lung abscesses heal and blood clotting disorders disappear, He could also cure stage IV cancer.

October was a month of steady progress. Kailen re-enrolled in classes and began her externships, she started radiation treatments at UK, and she accepted several speaking engagements. She shared her testimony of healing, hardship, and God's faithfulness at churches and even the UK College of Dentistry. She also continued writing and the TeamKCT blog was growing exponentially. Thousands of people from dozens of countries all over the world were now reading every post.

It was around this time that we began seeing cancer as a sort of eucatastrophe. What if God had actually used a cancer diagnosis to *heal* Kailen? It was, after all, the factor that had finally compelled her to have the colectomy, which had not only given her a life free of Crohn's Disease, but had also healed the blood clotting disorders. We were starting to believe it.

But the bigger question was this: What if God was using Kailen's cancer diagnosis to heal *others*?

Her testimony was changing the world. People saw this beautiful young woman suffering and dying in the prime of her life and thought what a shame it was, what a horrible God-forsaken situation. Then they read the blog or heard her speak. And the message they heard was not "woe is me" but rather "how great is my God." They listened in awe as she praised Jesus in the midst of terrible suffering.

There's no question Kailen changed the world, but she did it one person at a time. One such person was her own papaw, Prentys Combs, who upon admiring Kailen's inscrutable courage and hearing her battle-tested proclamations of faith, gave his life to Jesus at the age of 75.

Another example comes from her externship rotation at the VA hospital. For Kailen, every pain and every loss created an opportunity.

She had what JRR Tolkien might call, "eucatastrophic perspective."

TeamKCT blog post (October 18th, 2013):

> *I've been so ready and excited to start working with real patients with real problems because of how I can relate with all I have been through.*
>
> *Just yesterday I saw a woman who'd had a mastectomy, multiple people who have had blood clots, people wearing compression stockings, and even a man with an ileostomy.*
>
> *In the case of that particular man, I actually saw his bag peeking out from under his shirt, so I asked his wife if he'd had his colon removed. She said he had colon cancer and abscesses in his stomach and had required many drains to get all the fluid out...sound familiar at all?!?!*
>
> *I listened and then told her some of my story. Turns out the man was very self-conscious*

about his ileostomy bag. So, when he was done with his appointment, I pulled him over to the side and pulled up the bottom of my shirt so he could see my bag...

I didn't think I'd ever say this, but seeing the look on his face, how encouraged he was knowing that some young girl could live and work with a bag just like his, it made it all worth it. Even to the point that I told God I would keep my bag forever if it meant I could encourage people like that every day.

Take time to talk and LISTEN, even if for just a moment. Sometimes that is truly all someone needs.

♥ ♥ ♥

Kailen had radiation to her chest wall five days a week for six weeks, a total of thirty treatments. She also had three spot treatments to each of the three bony metastases – her neck, her left hip, and her tailbone.

Despite causing fatigue and what equated to a bad sunburn on her chest, after everything she had been through, radiation was a breeze. She had her last spot treatment on December 6th and officially finished her externships just in time for Christmas break.

We enjoyed the holidays with family, both in LaGrange and Matanzas, then drove back to Lexington feeling like we had a new lease on life. I was entering the final semester of my third year of pharmacy school, which meant it was my last semester in the classroom, which more importantly meant – NO MORE BLOCK EXAMS SWEET HOLY NECTAR! But even bigger news was that Kailen was healthier than she had ever been and was officially on the job hunt.

She had earned an Associate's in certified medical assisting (CMA) with phlebotomy. And while it wasn't the doctorate she had always dreamed of, it was an incredibly versatile degree that afforded her a wide range of career options.

She had been a smash hit on her externships and word was spreading around town. She could have worked just about anywhere she wanted, but we'd had our eye on one particular office for over a year. It was a dermatology clinic close to our apartment; it was in a nice area, required a short commute, and offered competitive pay and great hours.

Kailen sent applications to a number of offices, including the dermatology dream job, and when she hadn't heard anything back by mid-January, she decided to take matters into her own hands.

It turned out to be a day that would live in infamy.

TeamKCT blog post (January 16th, 2014):

> *If you've ever been around me at Christmas, birthdays, or any other occasion where there is any gift giving involved, you know that I HATE waiting to give my gifts to people.*

> *Some call it impatience, but I like to look at it as an inability to delay joy. I also hate to delay*

Even if you don't.

the joy of opening my own gifts because hey, I just love to be happy.

Now, I have been looking at my potential job as a BIG present from God and not just one that is going to give me joy, but one that will also be wrapped in a pretty bow of much-needed income, 401k, and the stability that has definitely been lacking from my and Bryan's life. Needless to say, my inability to delay joy has been at an all-time high this past week, so I decided to do something about it.

I filled out my online application this past Friday and when I hadn't heard anything back by Tuesday, I decided to take matters into my own hands. I got out of bed, cranked up my workout playlist, and was going to pump myself up before heading over to the dermatology office, finding the hiring manager, and letting them know just how much I would love this job.

So there I was, almost ready, halfway through "Moves Like Jagger," when my phone rings. It was an 859 number and I immediately just knew it was the dermatology clinic asking me for an interview, and I thought, "How convenient, I'm already dressed."

I answered the phone and upon saying "Hello" I hear, "Hi Kailen, this is Dr. Feddock with your results from last week's PET scan..."

Kailen didn't get the job at the dermatology clinic. In fact, she would never work anywhere as a certified medical assistant.

The most recent PET scan, performed by Dr. Feddock, Kailen's radiation oncologist at UK, had once again revealed bad news. While the original cancer spots looked great, three new metastases had formed – two in her spine, T12 and L4, and another in her right ischium.

Infamy indeed.

The news certainly caught us off guard, but to say we were shocked would be histrionic. Recurrence is in the very nature of metastatic cancer. Frankly, despite our faith, we knew it would happen eventually. But not this soon. Not when we had such positive momentum.

Right when life was about to start, it started to end.

TeamKCT blog post (January 16th, 2014):

> *After I hung up the phone and turned off the music, I sat on the bed and stared at the wall. I wasn't thinking and I couldn't even begin to process what this was going to mean.*
>
> *I sat there for a while and found myself staring at our wedding portrait hanging in our bedroom. I saw two starry-eyed people smiling at the camera. I saw two naïve children who had no idea what "in sickness or in health" was going to mean in their marriage. I saw another lifetime I could barely remember...*
>
> *It seems that once again, just as things are*

Even if you don't.

> *about to normalize, they are all just falling apart.*

> *It seems that I am going to have to stop my progress and put everything on hold again. It seems that I cannot catch a break. And it seems that life has dealt me a pretty cruddy hand just as I thought I was in the clear.*

This is a rare glimpse into Kailen's humanity. She felt these things – the pain, the loss, the disappointment, the frustration – just like anyone else. The difference, as always, was in how she chose to respond to those feelings.

Instead of wallowing in self-pity and giving up, she spoke truth into the void. She let the peace of Christ permeate the pain, and in that peace, she found strength to keep walking.

TeamKCT blog post (January 16th, 2014):

> *I won't say that I am happy about this or that it didn't come out of nowhere, because it did. But I will say that this time, Bryan and I are not going to allow cancer to dictate how "normal" our life is.*

> *Things are not going to fall apart because God is my foundation and He is THE rock on which I stand. I will not stop my progress or put anything on hold because "suffering produces PERSEVERANCE; perseverance, character; and character, hope."*

I may not have been given much of a break, but I am stronger now than I have ever been and will fight with more hope and peace than ever before.

And even though this really is a pretty cruddy hand, God's strength is made perfect in my weakness. He will never leave me or forsake me; I will fight a good fight and finish the race; I will rejoice in the Lord always.

Again, I say, rejoice.

We moved our appointment with Dr. Williams up to the next week. He was very clear about what this meant: the cancer was progressing faster than anticipated, and if left untreated...well, we weren't going to leave it untreated.

He started Kailen on an oral chemotherapy called Xeloda. It had the potential to be just as effective as intravenous chemo, but it could be taken at home and had milder side effects. Kailen was also taking two different hormone blockers – a pill called Tamoxifen and an injectable called Faslodex.

Williams ordered bloodwork and told us the recurrence was likely explained by one of two things: one, the colectomy nightmare had caused too long of a gap between chemo and radiation and had given the cancer an opportunity to advance, or two, it had always been there on the sub-microscopic level, undetectable by the scans.

Even if you don't.

The real answer was neither.

He called us two days later with the results of the bloodwork. Despite both hormone blocking medications, Kailen's estrogen still wasn't being adequately suppressed. It was fueling the fire, and if we weren't careful, it was about to blaze out of control.

There was a deliberate pause on the line before he said, "The ovaries have to go."

Wars produce casualties. We were well-acquainted with loss by this point, but never before had something cut us so deeply. How do you willingly let a doctor cut out your future? How do you surgically remove your hopes and dreams? In our case, we either did it or there *was* no future; there *were* no hopes and dreams.

The thought of losing her ovaries broke Kailen in a way that even death couldn't. But even still, beneath the weight of the most staggering loss imaginable in this life, she used her agony as a platform from which to proclaim the goodness of God and encourage others.

TeamKCT blog post (January 27th, 2014):

> *I am sure most all of you are familiar enough with the human anatomy to understand that, as a young couple who hasn't even had a chance to try and have a family of our own, this news was quite devastating. And to be honest, it still is.*
>
> *I can barely talk about it, think about it, or share it with others before the tears start to well up. Of everything I have ever been through, it*

has always seemed like it was going to be ok because there was always some sort of solution. And if there wasn't, the negative aspects affected only me.

But this, this is different.

No ovaries means no biological children of our own. No ovaries means never getting to experience pregnancy. No ovaries means no biological grandchildren for my and Bryan's parents. No ovaries means a lot of letting go of hopes and dreams and excitement for the future. And it is something I have yet to fully accept.

Before I go any further, I have to say that I know Bryan and I can still have a family of our own. In fact, there may be children born right now that will find a home with us someday through adoption. Not being able to have biological children is not the end of the world and doesn't make adopting any less special...So if/when that day comes, I will not love that child any less than my own. But saying that the emotions of loss and grieving that come with not being able to have biological children can simply be swept under the rug, is just plainly not true.

Accepting that, barring a miracle, I will never be able to give my husband the children that he and I have both dreamt of for years...seems like nothing but negative to me. But when I find myself seeing only the negative, as I seem to have been doing continually for the

Even if you don't.

past few years, there is something that always helps.

Bryan and I like to call this "grand-scheming it."

When you are going through something difficult, it's easy to find yourself with tunnel vision. Seeing only what is directly in front of you is normal. It's human nature. The problem, however, comes when satan seizes the opportunity and capitalizes on our lack of perspective. He tries to keep our heads down and turned away from God; he makes problems seem bigger than they are. And suddenly, you have no idea how you'll ever move beyond the next step.

You know what I'm talking about? I know you've been there. We all have. But it is at this moment, when you feel you are sinking in quicksand and even one more step is impossible, that "grand-scheming it" comes into play. Let me show you:

It seems Bryan and I are in an impossible place. Cancer has come back and I'm only 23. Not good odds by medical standards.

I was about to get a job when all of this started happening again. Now I am having my ovaries removed and in human sight I will never be able to have my own children. I can picture being the girl at all my friends' baby showers and everyone wondering how I'm handling seeing someone else experience the joy I'll never have. It feels like God has let us down and I will never be healed of anything. I am having emotions of anger, injustice, and wondering why. It feels like even if I could keep going I would only get smacked in the face again by some other health issue...

See what I mean by tunnel vision?

It is so easy to slip farther and farther back into the tunnel and disappear from the light all together because a lot of it is true. But one of the biggest things I learned growing up is, "DO NOT believe ANYTHING the devil says, EVEN WHEN IT'S TRUE."

In the grand scheme, we are not even close to an impossible situation because nothing is impossible for God. In the grand scheme, I am only 23 and have had cancer but the name of God is bigger even than the name of cancer. In the grand scheme, I haven't been able to get a job yet but God's timing IS perfect and I have the rest of my life to work. In the grand scheme, Bryan and I will be parents to someone at some point and because that child will be who God has for us, our family will be blessed. In the grand scheme, I was created and GIVEN a life only because GOD chose to create me. The only reason I am taking this next breath is because the God of the universe allows me to. The only reason I exist is to bring glory to God, my Father.

Even if you don't.

The day I chose to give my life back to Him, I said, "I will worship You through every storm, over every mountain, no matter what the cost, no matter how painful, no matter if I do not understand, and no matter how dark the moment may be."

In the grand scheme, I will one day live for all eternity in Heaven, and until that day, I have only ONE shot at this life to give everything back to the Lord who gave me life in the first place...

I pray that God will show you the grand scheme in your own life, and that you may not be trapped in the devil's tunnel vision.

Amen.

It took exactly one consultation with a gynecological surgeon in Louisville to help us realize we were headed back to Mayo.

Kailen's medical chart was the size of a Dallas phone book and getting thicker all the time; after the colectomy complications, the inside of her abdomen was an unexplored labyrinth of scar tissue and misplaced organs. Ovary removal was going to be immensely delicate. And seeing as the Louisville surgeon was sweating like a kid in the principal's office, we said thanks but no thanks and called Kailen's oncologist at Mayo.

The oncologist put us in touch with the appropriate surgical team, and in typical Mayo fashion, we had a slew of appointments scheduled within the hour. On Sunday, February 2nd, Kailen and her parents flew to Rochester for the seventh time. Surgical consultations were set for Monday.

Meanwhile, I stayed home to finish up block exams. It was Super Bowl Sunday, so I ordered a pizza and watched the game on mute while I studied.

A few hours and a whole pizza later, the weather took a turn for the worst. They were forecasting several inches of snow, but around midnight I walked out to find the parking lot coated in ice.

The Row C Alliance was having a study party at Matt's apartment, which was within walking distance of the College of Pharmacy. They had been texting me for hours trying to get me to join and I had repeatedly declined, citing my need to focus. But as the ice changed over to snow, I realized if I didn't head over soon, getting to my exam at 8 AM was going to be treacherous if not impossible.

It turned out to be an eventful all-nighter, made more eventful by the email we received just before dawn: classes were cancelled due to inclement weather. Monday's exam had been pushed back to Tuesday.

The Alliance celebrated and beers were literally and voluminously poured, but I wasn't drinking. I wasn't celebrating at all, actually. Because if I couldn't take my exam until Tuesday, I would miss the surgery.

And I would have quit pharmacy school before I made Kailen go through that alone.

I've mostly refrained from using names thus far, but I must make an exception for Dr. Robert Kuhn. Dr. Kuhn is one of the world's leading pediatric pharmacists. Between his work at the hospital, teaching at the College, conducting research, publishing scholarly articles, and speaking at conferences, Dr. Kuhn's time is extremely valuable.

Which makes what he did for me all the more remarkable.

I emailed him at 5:45 in the morning. There were six inches of snow on the ground (which is a veritable blizzard by Kentucky standards; six inches in Rochester would be considered a dusting) and it was still snowing. Classes were cancelled. There was really no reason for Dr. Kuhn to respond.

But he did. At 5:50.

Four hours later, I sat in his office and took my exam. And when I turned it in, Dr. Kuhn prayed for me. A prestigious professor at a public university insisted he pray for my wife's healing, and from that day onward, I got weekly emails from Dr. Kuhn asking not only about Kailen's progress, but also about how I was holding up.

I flew to Rochester that evening. Thanks to a three-hour layover in Minneapolis, I didn't get to the hotel until almost midnight. Kailen was nearly asleep when I came in, so I kissed her and prayed before climbing into bed beside her.

It wasn't until my head hit the pillow that I realized I had only slept four hours in the last forty-eight, and despite the overwhelming exhaustion, I was restless.

I tossed and turned until the alarm went off, marking the beginning of the first worst day of our lives.

As expected, surgery was complicated. The gynecological surgeon ended up having to tag-team the procedure with Rembrandt.

Laparoscopic techniques weren't possible due to the scar tissue accumulation in Kailen's abdomen, so they opened her up yet again, forming a long incision from her pubic bone to her navel. Rembrandt removed the internal drain that had been used to empty the loculated abscesses and sewed up the rectal stump, for what we hoped to God would be the final time. The gynecological surgeon then went in and extricated Kailen's ovaries and fallopian tubes.

The official title of the operation was salpingo-oophorectomy, which is an ostentatious name for the medical abolition of female fertility.

What it really was, of course, was a future-ectomy: a premeditated loss of life.

One of the more sadistic malevolencies of cancer is that, to have any hope of living, you must move perpetually closer to death. We infuse ourselves with expensive poisons that rob us of our hair and our humanity; we cut out organs and lop off limbs like we're bartering with the disease – a breast for six more months or maybe an ovary for a year. In effect, we are giving up actual life in exchange for the hope of life, trading a vibrant future for a stale present.

It's a fool's game that no one wins, but when you're dying, you have no choice but to play.

We were in the hospital for two days after the surgery. As always, we did our best to make fun where there was none. Jeff and I scoured Rochester, looking for unique food to bring back to the hospital for lunch and dinner; I bought Kailen books and coffee and souvenirs from our Barnes and Noble; we watched Kentucky basketball and even created our own basketball game in the room, creatively employing gauze, medical tape, and a vomit tub.

We did our best, but the melancholy cloak was tighter this time, the pain more deeply-rooted than ever before.

On a positive note, there were no dramatic post-surgical complications. Kailen was in some pain, mild for her standards, and was battling intermittent nausea, but overall she was healing up nicely. The incision looked great and there were no signs of infection. Once she was able to eat solid food and keep it down, the surgeon was willing to discharge her.

We left the hospital around 10 AM and spent the rest of the day at the hotel. Kailen stayed in bed most of the afternoon, watching *Friends* and various cooking shows on TV. Though she was still nauseous and taking pain meds as needed, she felt pretty good.

I watched her grimace a few times, but it wasn't from physical pain. It was in the moments when she realized the weight of what had just happened, as her soul slowly came to terms with what her mind already knew.

That night, she looked over at me and said, "I gotta get outta here."

After hours of sitting in bed, buried beneath the pain, the hotel room had become a stifling emotional prison. So we put her in a wheelchair, wrapped her tightly in one of the hotel comforters, and rolled her out into the frigid night air.

We left the hotel with no particular destination in mind, but when we heard music booming from Peace Plaza, we headed that direction. What we found was a sparkling display of ice sculptures and a huge crowd of people.

It was an event called Social ICE. Basically, it was an outdoor bar scene where everything was made of actual and literal ice. And when I say everything, I mean *everything* – the glasses, the chairs, the benches, the tables, and even the bars themselves. The entirety of Peace Plaza had seemingly been chiseled out of one massive ice block. And seeing as the temperature was fifteen below zero, it was a perfect evening to predicate festivities on all things frozen.

Kim and Kailen ordered hot chocolate, and while they went to find an ice-bench close to one of the many tower heaters set up around the Plaza, Jeff and I ordered something a little stronger.

We huddled close together, drank our drinks, and tried to let the unfailing quirkiness of Rochester wash away our pain. It worked, momentarily, and we each had another drink before Kailen started shivering and I rolled her back to the hotel.

Once Kim and Kailen were set up in the room, snuggled together watching a movie, Jeff and I decided to go find dinner. We made a quick pit stop and drank a beer, then stopped by the ice bar for another bourbon on our way to Newt's, Rochester's most famous burger joint. We ordered the food to-go and had another drink or two at the bar while we waited.

After making the briefest of stops at the ice bar on our way back, I was feeling the soothing warmth of alcohol for the first time in my life. We carried the food into the room and when I tripped and fell over onto the bed, Kailen gave me a strange look, then started belly laughing.

Realizing what we'd done, Kim slapped Jeff in the side of the head, then we were all laughing.

I learned quickly that greasy food tastes like the nectar of the gods when you've been drinking. I inhaled my burger and fries, all while blabbering drunken words that kept Kailen in hysterics.

I had thought maybe she would be mad at me, but it turned out to be quite the opposite. She *loved* it. Not because she wanted me to be drunk, or because she found it entertaining – though she certainly did – but because she knew the alcohol had temporarily whisked away the agony of reality.

She watched me laugh and joke and stumble around and saw me as I could have been, as I *should* have been, as a young man free of grief's burden.

(Some much-needed backstory: I was raised a straight-laced, stiff-collared, southern Baptist. And for the most part, I still adhere to those principles. But when I first met Kailen, I was downright pious. My straight laces and stiff collar defined me; they made me holy and obedient, but they also made me arrogant and unapproachable, utterly strangling my witness as a follower of Christ.

I had always been praised for my liturgical staunchness. My discipline was a point of pride, to say the least. So when I met Kailen, I puffed up my chest and told her I had never-not-once-no-not-ever had a sip of anything fermented and I no-not-ever would.

She responded with, and I quote, "*So?*"

She was wholly unimpressed, but more than that, she was disappointed. She certainly wasn't a party girl, and being underage, she too had never consumed alcohol. But she had always dreamed of having wine with her husband, or maybe enjoying some exotic drink under an umbrella on her honeymoon.

Scripture didn't outlaw alcohol, she told me. It merely taught that drunkenness was wrong. While I couldn't argue with her, my dogmatism and pride refused to yield. I was Bryan Taylor, stoically unalcoholic.

Fast forward two years: Kailen has methodically

deconstructed my stoicism. She has taught me that the purpose of life is to bring others to Christ by being *like* Christ, not by embodying the very characteristics most non-believers despise. There was nothing holy or Christ-like about my piety. It was, in fact, deeply unattractive, and served to cast those around me closer to moral nihilism than toward Christ.

She was right, of course, and this time around, my pride finally broke.

In September of 2012, less than a week before Kailen was diagnosed with cancer, she came home from class to find a bottle of blueberry wine and two long-stemmed glasses sitting on our kitchen table.

I had also left a note that read, "Will you please enjoy this with me?"

She cried. My humility was quite possibly the most meaningful display of love I had ever shown her, and together, we did the very thing I would no-not-ever do: *we sipped wine*.)

So, that night in the hotel, Kailen laughed until she was blue in the face as Kim took me through a field sobriety test. I failed fantastically, more square-dancing than actually walking a straight line, all the while proclaiming that I had "nailed it!"

An hour later, with Kailen's blessing, Jeff and I left again. We swung by the ice bar on our way to Chester's, a small restaurant downtown that had what we were after.

By this point I wasn't just intoxicated, I was rip-roarin' *drunk*. I knew drunkenness was wrong, but the wind chill was minus-thirty in Minnesota, my wife was dying, and I'd just lost the ability to have children. So I had another drink. Then another. And another. And then somewhere between eleven and fourteen more.

Once sufficiently socially lubricated, I became best friends with the guy sitting next to me. His name was Ron and he looked just like Sam Elliott, white mustache included.

Ron was visiting Rochester in remembrance of his wife, who had died from brain cancer at Mayo ten years ago to the day. I told Ron about Kailen and we took turns buying each other drinks, slipping ever further into alcohol-induced anesthesia.

Sometime during my last half dozen whiskeys, it occurred to me that, someday, I would become Ron: *Sitting in a bar on a cold night, drinking to simultaneously remember and forget the wife I once had, the life that could have been.*

It was a horrible fate, but as I watched Ron drain another beer, I realized I was powerless to stop it.

The walk back to the hotel was foggy. And though I was vaguely aware that Jeff was somewhere in my vicinity, the streets felt vacant. The temperature had dropped even further and a thin crystalline layer of frost had formed all over everything. As I stumbled along, I wondered if maybe this was what dying was like: a dark, cold, cumbersome stroll through a lonely tube of shimmering darkness, with nothing but the fading hope of eternity to save you from oblivion.

I was still pondering that oblivion when Jeff shoved me, sparing me a shin-first collision with a fire hydrant.

I nodded my gratitude and eventually staggered through the hotel lobby to the elevators. We parted ways outside his room, and after fumbling with the key card for quite some time, I eventually made it to mine.

Kailen was asleep, albeit sitting up to avoid putting pressure on the incision, and she stirred without waking when I came in. I brushed my teeth, or at least I hope I did, and sat down on the room's other bed to avoid further disturbing her.

I was too nauseous to lay flat so I just sat there and watched her sleep, trying not to heave the contents of my stomach onto the cheap paisley comforter, and imagined the wonderful mother she would never be to the children we would never have.

We flew home on Friday.

The flight was uncomfortable for Kailen, but nothing like the horrid experience after colectomy, and when we got back to Rupp and Layla, the melancholic fog slowly began to lift. A group of friends came over on Saturday, many of whom we hadn't seen in months, and life felt relatively good.

Kailen still wasn't able to eat much, a byproduct of nausea and a very sore abdomen, but she allowed herself a small snack after everyone left. It was fully within the dietary restrictions imposed by the surgeons. But three hours later, she woke up to go to the bathroom and realized none of the food had passed through the ileostomy.

She wasn't worried and didn't even wake me, but when she couldn't fall back asleep, she started feeling chilled. She took her temperature and when I heard the thermometer beep, I rolled over.

Her eyes told the story; she had spiked a fever of 102. Our post-surgery instructions were to immediately report to the emergency room if her temperature ever exceeded 100.3.

We stared at each other as a familiar dread descended upon us.

How could this be happening again?

We called the on-call physician at Mayo. He was clearly concerned, but when we expressed our desperate desire to avoid yet another ER visit, he told us to sleep on it until morning. If the food still hadn't passed and the fever hadn't broken, we would have no choice.

We thanked him and eventually willed ourselves back to sleep.

We slept a fitful two hours before everything fell apart. Kailen woke with apoplectic pain raging through her stomach and groin. She gingerly rolled out of bed and limped to the bathroom, her body hunched over at the waist, and laid on her back, writhing in agony.

Even if you don't.

I sat with her for a while, but when she started vomiting, I knew we couldn't wait any longer.

I packed our bags, loaded up the dogs, and we drove back to Louisville. We checked into the ER around 5:00 AM and by 7:00, they had performed a deluge of tests and scans. Nothing was definitive, but the doctor said the abdominal CT showed something called "stranding" in Kailen's stomach. It could mean a number of things, he explained, but with Kailen's history, it was likely the beginnings of another infection.

We were allowed to go back to Kim and Jeff's to shower and clean up, but then it was right back to Norton Brownsboro. We stayed the night in the hospital so Kailen could be continuously monitored. I sat at a small desk and studied most of the night because that was more pleasant than trying to sleep on the couch-bed. Then, a little before dawn, I sat by the window and watched it snow.

I didn't feel well, and the thought occurred to me that maybe it had something to do with not sleeping for the past week. It was unfortunate, but there was no sense in complaining or worrying about it; it was what it was, and there was no end in sight.

Kim and Jeff picked us up around 6:00 and we headed to the airport.

After just twenty-four hours at home, and less than three hours of sleep, we were flying back to Mayo. Again.

With an abdominal abscess. *Again.*

179

We were direct admitted into Rochester Methodist Hospital on Monday afternoon, but weren't seen by the surgical team until Tuesday morning rounds.

Kailen was still NPO, which meant she hadn't eaten or had anything other than water to drink since that fateful Saturday night snack. Three days without food is enough to make anyone cranky, even Kailen. So when one of the doctors came in and jokingly asked why we had been so eager to see him again, Kailen just stared at him, her implication obvious: *shut up and get me out of here.*

This particular room didn't even have a couch-bed, so I was sprawled contortedly in a cheap plastic recliner, my spine beginning to resemble a slinky. It was now approaching two weeks since I'd last had a full night's sleep. Needless to say, I didn't laugh at the doctor's cute little joke either.

But despite our gloomy moods, the news was actually stellar: there was no abscess.

Kailen had something called an ileus, which is essentially a temporary paralysis of the bowel. The doctors told us it was common after abdominal surgery and other forms of trauma. In Kailen's case, a short segment of her small intestine had become dormant, preventing her from passing food. The intestinal backflow had then caused the searing stomach pain, the nausea, and the fever.

We were extremely relieved and grateful, but the

frustration didn't just immediately melt away. After ovary removal, we were in desperate need of normality, something, *anything*, to stabilize the turbulence. An all-night ER visit, our eighth flight to Mayo, and three more restless nights in a hospital weren't exactly what we had in mind.

It was salt on an open wound. But at least everything was okay and now we could go home, right?

Wrong.

A massive ice storm was blasting the south. Mississippi, Alabama, and Georgia had all sustained record ice accumulations, bringing all forms of transportation, and life in general, to an abrupt halt. The southeastern hub was in complete gridlock; flying anywhere south of Chicago was a virtual impossibility. We were grounded in Rochester until Friday at the absolute earliest.

It was more bad news we didn't need. But to be honest, it was almost comical at that point. We were tired and we were hurting, but as always, we chose to make the best of it. Once Kailen's ileostomy started functioning again, she was discharged and we had the rest of the week to enjoy Rochester.

We found new restaurants and explored new items at some of our usual haunts – Pannekoeken, City Café, Newt's, Chester's, McGoon's, Pescara, and City Market. Kim and Kailen got their nails done, Jeff and I found a unique clothing store with all kinds of exotic dress shirts and sport coats, and of course, we frequented our Barnes and Noble at the Chateau

Theater. I even made friends with the pharmacist at Eagle Drug, a family-owned pharmacy that had been a staple in the heart of downtown for almost ninety years.

Though we often experienced it during trauma, Rochester was sort of magical. It often felt like an enchanted land disjointed from the rest of reality, like we had somehow gotten on a plane in Louisville and accessed a parallel universe. It was the Mayberry of the North, more a state of mind than an actual place. Looking back, I realize what an incredible gift it truly was.

We ended up having a great week, a kind of pseudo-vacation, and when the south finally thawed out, we flew home.

This time there were no complications and life truly did blend back into normality. I caught up with my classes and Kailen finally started recovering from the ovary procedure in earnest.

Routines were critically important to both of us, partly because they appealed to our meticulous tendencies, but mostly because living within a habitual construct was the only way to trick ourselves into believing we had a normal life.

Following that eighth trip to Mayo, we established a new one. The full healing process took about six weeks, but Kailen didn't sit idle. While I immersed myself in the final few months of the spring semester, she focused on knitting, reading, cooking, maintaining the blog, and of all things, physical fitness.

She wasn't allowed to lift anything heavier than ten pounds until the full six weeks was up, but she modified her TIU workouts so she could start back right away. TIU didn't ultimately save her life, but in so many ways, it *gave* her life. Her dedication to the daily workouts and the nutritious meal plan accelerated her healing, and by early March, Kailen was feeling better than she ever had, even before cancer.

If I hadn't known better, I would have thought she was healed.

We enjoyed a triumphant *bird-day breffust* on her 24th birthday (her *golden* birthday – if you knew Kailen, you knew this was a big deal), we went on the trip-of-a-lifetime to Marco Island with her family (in Jeff's words, "what we had been through was not normal, so our vacation wasn't going to be normal either"), then a few weeks later were lucky enough to go watch Kentucky play in the Sweet Sixteen and Elite Eight in Indianapolis.

When Aaron Harrison hit the game-winning shot to beat Louisville, we yelled and screamed, I bit off a large chunk of one of my teeth, we kissed, then we yelled and screamed some more.

For the first time in a long time, the world felt right: Kailen was as healthy as she had been in a decade, pharmacy school was nearing its end, and Kentucky had just defeated the worst team on earth.

My final round of finals ended just before Easter and we celebrated our victory over block exams. But as our celebrations so often were, it was cut short. Kailen had a PET scan and several MRIs on Thursday and Saturday before Easter, and on Monday, we had our monthly check-up appointment with Dr. Williams.

As you might have guessed, the news wasn't good.

Despite everything we had done to fight the cancer – IV and oral chemotherapy, months of radiation, hormone suppressors, colectomy, mastectomy, salpingo-oophorectomy – it was *still* winning.

TeamKCT blog post (April 29th, 2014):

> *We checked in, got back to the room, in walks my doctor, and I knew as soon as I saw his face.*
>
> *Then he said the words we prayed we wouldn't hear. He said the words that haven't stopped repeating over and over in my head ever since.*
>
> *"Your numbers are up and your scans don't look good."*
>
> *"Your numbers are UP and your scans DON'T look good."*
>
> *"YOUR numbers are UP and YOUR scans DON'T look good."*
>
> *My heart stopped. He went right into showing us my PET and MRIs and explained exactly what they saw going on.*

Even if you don't.

Apparently, there are several more spots throughout my spine and hips in addition to the spots that were in my bones previously. They aren't huge, but they are definitely showing up on the scans, and the fact that anything is progressing when we've already taken so many steps is very concerning.

I was on hormone blockers, I had my ovaries removed, and I'm still taking a drug for hormonal therapy. And yet, my body is still somehow finding a way to kill itself.

Why? We don't know yet.

I know that sounds harsh, but it's the truth. There is something in my body that is trying to destroy me, and so far, we haven't been able to fully suppress it.

It's a sobering thought, and today I have had a lot of that "ew, ew get it off me" feeling I had with the tumor in my breast.

Only this time, I can't really imagine them removing my spine...

It wasn't so much a revelation as it was a reminder: *Cancer never quits.*

It's made of "us," and just like us, it has an indwelt will to live. It's resourceful and clever, recalcitrant, stubbornly unfastidious, taking advantage of even the narrowest window of opportunity. Yet again, the cancer in Kailen's bones had found some fractional quantity of estrogen and latched onto it for dear life. In spite of every estrogen-blocking modality we had employed, we still couldn't eliminate it completely.

The news was devastating, like cancer recurrences always are, but this time, Kailen and I refused to wallow in the devastation. Our newfound routine and sense of rightness in the world had been purchased at a high price; we weren't about to let a bad scan undo all our hard work.

Dr. Williams tweaked Kailen's medication regimen again and we pushed ahead.

In keeping with our yearly theme, that summer was sublime. Kailen continued pounding away at her TIU workouts and by mid-June, we were back in the gym together. I was in the midst of fourth-year rotations, which meant I more or less had a normal work day. I went to my rotation, worked for eight to ten hours, then came home and actually lived like a regular human being.

No studying. No all-nighters. No office quarantines.

Instead, we started going on walks again, taking the dogs back through Andover, like we had done before the war. We ate popsicles on the steps. And in brief moments, gliding through the heat-soaked dusk, we even let ourselves dream again.

Kailen's next round of PET scans were far from miraculous, but they weren't catastrophic either, which we interpreted as reason to celebrate. We walked the dogs across Man-O-War Boulevard and bought ice cream, savoring the sweetness of summertime. They were some of the best days of our life, and we knew it.

July was a month of milestones. Kailen was now running every day, completely unimpeded by her health. We even went hiking at Red River Gorge, something she thought she would never be able to do. She continued her ardent dedication to TIU and was now able to lift weights at the gym. Her transformation from February was astounding, in both body and spirit.

On July 4th, we went to a fireworks party with friends and Kailen didn't have to sit anything out. She played whiffle ball, Can-Jam, and corn-hole, and even jumped on the trampoline.

For the first time in her life, she felt like everyone else.

Though we both knew the reprieve was likely temporary, Kailen continued holding fast to her faith in miracles. She never once doubted that God *could* heal her; He could heal her completely and totally and forever.

In the face of all medical knowledge and earthly doubt, Kailen's faith in the God of miracles was undeterred.

TeamKCT blog post (July 3rd, 2014):

> *I will not stop bombarding the gates of Heaven for my miracle!*

> *I believe with ALL of my heart that God is my*

healer and that He can clear my body 100% of any cancer cell that may be trying to destroy me.

I mean, think about it. If He can wipe us all clean of every sinful action, thought, intention, or emotion we have ever had?...

Hello people, cancer don't stand a chance!

It takes courage to maintain that kind of faith, to continually open yourself up to disappointment, to stare down the reality of false hope and keep hoping all the same. Kailen had more courage than any person I've ever known, and by the beginning of August, it was about to be put to the test yet again.

For it was nigh time for our annual autumnal cataclysm.

I've heard it said that pain is a universal language.

In all candor, I find that to be a complete load of horse crap. No one is without pain, but not all pain is created equal.

Bobby stubs his toe while Jimmy battles metastatic bone cancer that makes it feel as though someone is chinking away at his skeleton with an ice pick. I'd like to promulgate the theory that, while Bobby and Jimmy are both experiencing pain, they are definitely not experiencing the same thing. It's a simple fact that a person speaking English and a person speaking French are not speaking the same language; the same principle applies to pain.

By August 2014, Kailen had already endured a lifetime's worth of physical agony. Her pain tolerance was so high it actually posed a medical problem, making it impossible to tell whether she was hurting or not. She had contended with daily stomach pain most of her life, dislocated ribs, numerous surgeries, radiation burns, and a three-liter abscess in her abdomen.

It all hurt, but nothing compared to the meteoric anguish of bone pain.

Like most of our traumatic experiences, it started during the night. I woke to a faint popping sound. I sat up and looked around, even got out of bed and checked the living room to make sure someone hadn't broken in. But when I came back into the bedroom, I realized the source of the noise:

Kailen's teeth were chattering.

"I'm okay," she whispered. But I knew she wasn't. I sat on the side of the bed and felt her forehead – she was burning up. The pain was so great it was precipitating a fever.

"Where does it hurt, sweetie?" I asked.

She winced and her eyes filled with tears. "My back."

The cancer in her spine was rearing its ugly head, and when we checked into the hospital the next morning, Dr. Williams didn't look surprised. He had known it was only a matter of time.

Cancer in the bone, he told us, is one of the most painful things on earth. As the cancer progresses, it literally eats away the bone like acid on a penny. It's voracious, and though its momentum can often be slowed with medicine or radiation, it can never be fully stopped.

Kailen could barely move without sending white-hot tendrils up her spine into her brain. Even breathing hurt. Dr. Williams increased her pain medication significantly, and a few days later, with the screaming pain muffled to a whisper, we were allowed to leave.

Though the misery had abated some, there was no relief in sight. Kailen was still hurting every minute of every day, and despite being discharged, we drove straight back to the hospital. Only this time, it wasn't for Kailen.

Kim had been hospitalized again. After what everyone had hoped would be a routine gallbladder surgery, Kim was suddenly in the ICU. By the time we arrived, she was already on the ventilator, fighting for her life.

Her gallbladder had been so infected it had become gangrenous. The doctors didn't discover it until it was too late and Kim had fallen into septic shock. To make matters much worse, an unforeseen heparin allergy sprung a number of blood clots, which resulted in Kim having a heart attack and going into full renal failure.

She was in the hospital for over a month, from July 29th through September 2nd, and very nearly died. Thankfully, she pulled through just in time for Kailen to be readmitted.

The pain was back with unrestrained fury. It had spread from her spine to her hips and was making her whole body tremble. She couldn't eat, drink, sleep, or bathe; the pain had consumed everything.

Though Dr. Williams had expected our situation to get worse, he didn't expect it quite so quickly. It had only been three weeks since he increased her medication and he was already increasing it again. That could only mean one thing: *disease progression.*

It was a long night, even longer than usual, and the next morning Kailen woke up with a new symptom – her right eye was swollen.

When Dr. Williams came by on rounds, he said it was probably just the way she had slept. But later in the day, he seemed to re-think his opinion and sent her down for a scan.

The pain intensified throughout the afternoon, and by the time Williams came by with the results, Kailen had been given enough intravenous narcotics to sedate an elephant. She was barely conscious, much less coherent enough to have a cogent conversation, so Dr. Williams pulled up a chair and talked to me.

"This isn't good," he said. "The cancer has spread to her orbital bone. That's the cause of the swelling."

I looked over at her lying in bed, her eye almost swollen shut. Seeing her beautiful face contorted in such a vile way broke something inside me. She was so innocent, so pure, so undeserving of such defilement.

I wanted to cry but couldn't; everything in me had dried up.

"We'll need to do a full-body PET in the morning," he continued. "But until then, don't tell her anything. Just let her rest."

"What does this mean?" I asked.

"Palliative radiation and chemo as soon as possible," he said, then met my eyes before repeating, "This isn't good, Bryan."

I carried that burden quietly the rest of the night. I assumed Kailen hadn't registered anything Williams said, because when Alex Weires showed up to visit later that evening, Kailen insisted they get up and dance.

No, I'm actually not joking.

She literally got up and danced to Meghan Trainor's *All About That Bass*. Kim and I videoed it on our phones and it quickly went viral throughout the hospital. Pretty soon we had nurses from other floors stopping by just to catch a glimpse of the terminal cancer patient so filled with joy she had to dance.

Hours later, after everyone left, I was lying on the couch-bed staring at the ceiling, wondering how I was going to tell my wife that cancer had invaded her face. How would I explain to her that the war was about to start all over again?

There were no answers. The room was deathly quiet until, suddenly, she spoke.

"Do you think I'll make it to Christmas?"

I rolled over, stunned. She hadn't moved. In fact, her eyes weren't even open. But she repeated her question.

"Babe, do you think I'll make it to Christmas?"

I didn't know if she was talking out of her head or if she had actually heard everything.

Nonetheless, I confidently replied, "Yes, baby, you will."

She didn't say anything else because she had already fallen back asleep, but her question haunted me the rest of the night. Her words had been heavily slurred and I realized there was no way she could have actually understood Dr. Williams. She didn't know the cancer was back, that it had spread all over her body. I was going to have to tell her.

I don't think I slept at all, and when sunlight finally streamed in through the blinds, something strange happened. For the first and only time in my life, I heard God speak audibly. It came from everywhere and nowhere, like an echo with no source.

"Don't envy Me," He whispered.

Though His words were mysterious, I immediately understood what He meant. As a new day dawned, I already knew the horrors the day would hold. I knew that in about an hour, Kailen would wake up in pain and I would have to explain everything. I would have to watch the realization reach her eyes, and for a moment, I would be the one inflicting the pain. I had the ability to see the future, and it hurt worse than anything I had ever experienced.

"Don't envy Me," God said again.

I realized this was the weight He had carried since the dawn of creation. This agony was what He felt all the time. He always knew what was coming; for Him, the pain was constant.

When she woke up, finally lucid, I told her the truth. It was just as bad as I'd imagined, and after that, I was never the same.

♥ ♥ ♥

A few hours later, they loaded Kailen back down with narcotics and we took a short ambulance ride across the street to the imaging center.

The full-body PET scan took a while, so I stepped outside and called Dr. Anne Policastri, the rotation coordinator at the College of Pharmacy. Dr. Policastri was already well-acquainted with my and Kailen's situation, so when I told her things had taken a turn for the worst, she instantly put me at ease.

With chemo and radiation looming, and Kailen's

condition deteriorating, I knew I couldn't be away from her. Unlike the first time through chemo, this round seemed to portend an approaching collapse. She was going to need my equanimity more than ever; when she couldn't fight anymore, I intended to fight for her. And to do that, I had to be with her on a daily basis.

Dr. Policastri never asked for an explanation. She just worked her magic and got my vacation block switched, which afforded me the next six weeks to be with Kailen.

I was standing behind the imaging center, leaning against a chain-link fence, watching a silver maple shed its leaves into the parking lot when she told me. And as I thanked her for her kindness and understanding, I broke down. I was so hysterical I could barely even finish the conversation, and after we hung up I pressed my face against the fence and wept until my eyes were swollen and dry.

It was the last time I'd cry for almost eleven months.

The next day Dr. Williams told us the excruciating pain was coming from two primary sources: one, the cancer had once again spread and intensified. Kailen's spine and pelvis had lit up like a Christmas tree on the PET scan. And two, thanks to the cancer and ongoing hormone suppressive therapy weakening Kailen's bone integrity, she had sustained bilateral ischial fractures, meaning she had a broken bone in both hips. The fact that Kailen had remained conscious amid such torment was a miracle unto itself.

Radiation started that afternoon and lasted for two

weeks. Kailen had spot treatments to her orbital bone, spine, and pelvis, all meant to alleviate pain, and to whatever extent was still possible, eradicate disease.

After three or four days, the swelling in her eye was gone and the pain relief was enough to get us discharged. We stayed with Kim and Jeff and made the daily commute into the hospital for treatment.

At the end of the two weeks, the pain was dramatically improved and we were able to lower Kailen's narcotic dose, which allowed her to be herself again. She still walked with a cane, a result of the ischial fractures, but after enduring the agony of the last month, being able to walk at all was a gift.

We had a few days before our first chemo consultation with Dr. Williams and we spent them trying to relax and recover. That was when Kailen told me it was time.

"Time for what?" I asked, a little nervous.

"Time to get tattoos," she said.

She had been talking about wanting a tattoo ever since diagnosis, but to be honest I never thought we'd actually do it. Until cancer, Kailen and I weren't really tattoo-type people. But then again, before Kailen, I didn't drink either.

Life has a satirical way of humbling you.

That night, we got tattoos. And in a display of solidarity, so did Kristen and Jarrod.

Even if you don't.

Jarrod got a cross with "TeamKCT" inscribed on his shoulder, Kristen got the famous words from the old hymn, "It is Well with My Soul", on her side, and I had my and Kailen's battle creed written on the inside of my left bicep, stenciled in Kailen's own handwriting:

Stay in the Fight.

When it came time for Kailen to choose, there were countless scriptures and expressions of faith that were significant to her, but the decision was easy. There was only one phrase that best defined her soul: from the lung collapse on the first night of her life, to Crohn's disease, blood clots, abscesses, and stage IV cancer, Kailen had always maintained a simple answer to life's most complicated question:

What if God doesn't?

What if God doesn't heal my colon? What if He doesn't bring me the husband I've always prayed for? What if He doesn't bless me with children of my own? What if He doesn't take away the pain? What if He doesn't stop the cancer from killing me? What if He doesn't perform any of the miracles I've asked Him to perform?

What if He doesn't? What then?

She wrote her answer on her left forearm, for all the world to see:

Yet I Will Praise Him.

197

On October 5th, we had our second TeamKCT Haircutting Party. Jeff, Jarrod, and I shaved our heads again, Kailen and Kristen got pixie cuts, and this time, our friends came.

Chemo started a week later and we were finally able to move back to Lexington. Her condition was steadily improving but her prognosis wasn't, so I used my newfound free time to house hunt.

One of Kailen's greatest dreams in life was to have her own home, a place where she could nest and cook and decorate. She was deeply ambitious, but in her heart, she wanted nothing more than to be a homemaker and a mother. I had long ago realized my purpose in life was to make as many of her dreams come true as possible in the short time we had left, and though I would never be able to make Kailen a mother, I was intent on giving her a home to make.

Growing up, Kailen's family moved around a lot. She had lived in almost a dozen different houses in a handful of cities, but there was one ever-present feature that always identified a place as home: *a willow tree.*

It seems statistically improbable, but every place she'd ever lived had a willow somewhere on the property, including our apartment in Lexington.

Kailen had a unique way of communicating with God, a poetic connection with her Creator that undergirded everything she did, and I'll forever see the willow as a symbol of that divinely eccentric conversation.

Even if you don't.

In late October, a friend sent me a link to a house in Frankfort. I wasn't interested at first; the picture made it look shoddy and rundown. But considering moving to Frankfort would get us thirty minutes closer to Kailen's doctors, I swung by and checked it out.

The picture was accurate – it *was* shoddy and rundown, a ranch style brick structure that hadn't been updated since it was built in the 60's. Surrounding it were other houses just like it, some older, some newer, but for the most part, the neighborhood was a well-preserved relic of the Cold War.

I almost didn't even get out of the car; there was an untrimmed tree in the front yard cascading branches haphazardly over the house and driveway, making the property nearly inaccessible. But when I realized what kind of tree it was, I killed the ignition and opened my door.

Despite the house needing some serious work, it had a large fenced-in backyard ideal for Rupp and Layla. There was also an expansive back porch, a garage, and the street was secluded and quiet.

Given the presence of the willow tree standing guard out front, I had little choice but to call the number listed on the website.

Once I brought Kailen by to see the place, the decision was made. She loved it. Because unlike me, she had a vision for what it could be. The fact that it was so weathered actually made it better; it was a blank canvas, which allowed her to put her full creative ability on display.

I signed the lease a few days later and we immediately got to work. We cleaned the house, painted the walls, mowed the yard, and trimmed the trees, giving new life to the property. Kim and Jeff were generous enough to help us buy furniture and all the items Kailen needed to stamp her artistic flare on the place.

In less than a week, we moved into our new home and Kailen gave her most poignant form of approval: *she squealed.*

I started back on rotations in November and Kailen's chemo regimen continued, three weeks on, one week off. The chemo was more potent this time, and thus so were the side effects; she battled constant fatigue and persistent nausea, but with the pain mostly under control, we established yet another new routine.

My first rotation was in Frankfort, just down the road from our house, and for six weeks, we lived like Ward and June Cleaver. I woke up early and built her a fire in the fireplace, made a pot of coffee, we had breakfast together, and by the time I got home she had dinner ready.

It was idyllic not because it was spectacular or extravagant, but because it was normal. It was our finite version of the American dream.

First came Thanksgiving, then Christmas, and I spent what little money I had to buy Kailen nice things for our home. When she opened up the Kitchen-Aid mixer I got her for our anniversary, she cried, then took it straight to the kitchen and started making cookies.

Even if you don't.

We made our yearly trek to LaGrange and Matanzas, then travelled back home with the prayer that the new year would bring a revitalized hope of healing and restoration.

It started off well enough. I finished another rotation, Kailen was done with three full rounds of chemo, and we were prepared to move to Ohio County for six weeks while I completed a rotation in Madisonville.

Everything went according to plan until early February, when Kailen's right leg started to swell.

As you might imagine, our first concern was that she had another blood clot.

We called Dr. Williams right away, but when we described the symptoms, he assured us it wasn't a DVT. It was something called lymphedema, a condition where lymph fluid escapes the lymph vessels and floods the interstitial space, causing swelling. In our case, palliative radiation to Kailen's right hip had injured a series of lymph nodes, leading to damaged vessels and the resultant edema.

You might think it was a relief to discover she didn't have a blood clot, and I suppose it was, but the lymphedema was horrible in its own way. Her leg swelled up so badly she wasn't able to walk or even stand for long periods of time. It made sleeping difficult because of the pressure it put on her hip, which then led to pain in her back.

It was a small thing in comparison to everything else, but when *combined* with everything else, it was downright torturous. We started seeing a lymph specialist who taught us how to massage her leg and wrap it to help manage the swelling; the relief was minimal and Kailen grudgingly went back to wearing my old baseball sweatpants, just as she had done after colectomy.

It's tough to describe what happened next.

We were in Ohio County and Kailen was only two chemo treatments away from getting a month break. Despite the lymphedema, she was feeling better than she had in weeks. She went back to Louisville for a round of scans and spent the weekend with Alex Weires.

When it came time for church, Kailen didn't want to go because she didn't want to wear sweatpants in front of everyone, but Alex was unfazed. She simply put on sweatpants too, and together, they walked into Southeast Christian Church unashamedly.

It was during this church service that God gave Kailen a breath of fresh air. And, as always, His timing was perfect – because things were about to get a lot worse.

TeamKCT blog post (February 12th, 2015):

> *For the past three to four months, I have been in a funk. Big time.*
>
> *As of this past September and the second*

major attack of cancer on my body, Bryan and I have been in a battle.

We went through it in September of 2012 when cancer made its first strike and we spent the next year or so battling and recovering from all the ways cancer had wounded us. After the first round of chemo, radiation, colon removal, drains, mastectomy, drains, ovary removal, and more drains...we had a lot of scars.

My body was obviously very physically scarred, but we both had even deeper emotional and spiritual scars. Cancer takes so much from you, and after our year of walking through hell and back, we had a lot of recovering to do.

Then, this past September, when everything came back, we opened up those same scars all over again. And just like it hurts when a surgeon has to cut through layers and layers of scar tissue on a patient who has had previous surgeries, Bryan and I were suddenly realizing just how scarred we really were.

And it was painful.

My doctors told me the cancer was back, and a scar was ripped open. They told me I was going to have to do radiation again, and another scar was ripped open. The clippers took the first swipe of wispy curls off my head, and a scar through my heart was ripped open.

My freedom once again belonged to

treatments and hospitals and doctor visits, and a scar was ripped wide open. We had spent almost two years trusting God, praying healing over my body, believing, and then actually getting to enjoy some time when I was free from doctors, but then it all came back. It all came back and suddenly I was lying there a bloody mess as all my scars had been ripped open and exposed even deeper than they had been the first time.

I had no clue how to make sense of it all.

In many ways, I had taken one step forward and fifty steps back. Physically, emotionally, spiritually, and in how I trusted God.

I have always trusted God in everything. I've never really struggled with that, but all of a sudden, I found myself wanting to pull away. I guess you could say I was really offended. How could God do this to me? I already went through it once and had trusted Him all the way through.

Hello. I ALREADY WENT THROUGH IT ONCE AND HAD TRUSTED HIM ALL THE WAY THROUGH.

And yet, He let it happen again. I mean, where do you put that? What do you do with that? In your logical, philosophical, spiritual mind, where does that go?

My God, my own Father, who reached out

Even if you don't.

His hand to me and said, "Trust me. Do not be afraid. I will protect you under the shadow of my wings. By My stripes, you are healed. I will restore health to you and heal you of your wounds..."

He let cancer come back again.

At first, I kept walking with a smile on my face just like I did the first time around. Stubbornness kicked in and I figured, hey, I walked through it once, I can do it again. So I did, and it worked fine until I realized all I was doing was walking. I was waking up, taking my pills, hoping it was going to be a good day physically, and barely putting one foot in front of the other. It wasn't working anymore...

After this past September, I found myself walking much more cautiously with God and trying to do things in my own strength instead of depending fully on Him. And as we all know, that will only get you so far. As humans, we simply cannot go it alone in this world, and because I was trying to walk in my own strength, that is exactly how I found myself last week: feeling totally alone.

But lo and behold, that is when God finally chose to show Himself to me.

It happened at a church service last Saturday night...we were worshipping and I was sitting in my seat singing along. As I often do during worship, I looked up to the ceiling; it helps me remember that I am worshipping someone bigger than me and my problems.

So, I'm singing and staring at the ceiling when, suddenly, I could feel Him. I don't know how to explain it exactly, but it was the same way I always feel God, a quickening in my spirit.

Tears came to my eyes, I raised my hands, and then I just knew there were angels in the room with us. I tried so hard to see them with my physical eyes and never could, but I knew in my spirit that the Spirit of the Lord was in that place, and that angels were singing and worshipping with us. I could "see" them with their hands raised and their wings flapping in a grand and Heavenly manner; and as I watched their beating wings, I suddenly had to gasp.

It was like they were moving the air about the room and it was moving so fast I literally had to catch my breath. I inhaled as deeply as I could and felt a spirit of peace, renewal, and strength wash over me like a flood.

Remember when you were a kid and you jumped off the diving board and did a pencil? You went really far down into the deep end of the pool, touched the bottom, and then had to start kicking your way back up to the top. You kicked and kicked and when it looked like you were about to break through the surface, you didn't. You got a little panicky and kicked harder and just when you thought you couldn't

Even if you don't.

wait any longer for that next breath, you broke out of the water and gasped.

Well, for the past few months, the devil has been dragging me deeper and deeper under the water and I have been kicking and trying to get back to the surface. And it was that moment, sitting in my seat during worship, that God finally took me by the hand and pulled me back up.

I am SO thankful to have a renewed strength, hope, and trust in my Heavenly Father. Unfortunately, it seems He pulled me up just in time, because the results from the MRIs this past week were not the good results we were hoping for.

I had a PET scan week before last and it showed that all the cancerous activity in my body had responded well to the chemo. Nothing on the scan lit up except for one small spot on my neck and one tiny speck on my liver. My doctor wasn't sure if it was malignant or not, so just to be safe, he ordered an extra set of MRIs.

For some reason, the MRIs showed a lot more activity going on that didn't show up on the PET scan. We don't know all the details yet, but I have another MRI, a bone scan, and a liver CT scheduled for next week. Those tests will hopefully show us exactly what we are dealing with and will help my doctors know how we need to respond.

In the meantime, I wanted to let you know that we can all take a deep breath and continue to pray.

I pray the Lord gives each and every one of you a fresh gasp of His peace and strength that you may be able to dive back under the waters with us and do battle! We don't know exactly what we are facing yet, but we do know that no matter what it is, our God is ALWAYS stronger.

No matter how deep satan may try to pull me, just like we learned in the song as children, "Deep and wide, deep and wide, there's a fountain flowing deep and wide."

That fountain is His peace and that fountain is His healing.

Besides, I'm pretty sure my God can breathe underwater.

The week after the follow-up scans, it snowed a foot in Ohio County. Being a weather fanatic, I was pretty much in Heaven. I stayed up all night measuring and recording hourly accumulation rates and comparing them to historical values. Then, the next morning, I played in it like I was ten years old again.

It was the biggest snow of my lifetime (final tally was 17.5" in Matanzas), and while it allowed me to stay home from rotation and indulge my meteorological fantasies, it also prevented us from travelling to

Even if you don't.

Kailen's doctor's appointment in Louisville.

She was supposed to get a chemo infusion and hear the results of the scans. The delay between infusions was less than two weeks, but that was enough to trigger the avalanche.

On the day of the snow, Kailen began having back spasms and sharp pains in her abdomen. The lymphedema had gotten worse, so she was already walking with a cane, but now she had to hunch over to keep from stretching her stomach muscles, which in turn made the back pain worse.

When the spasms hit, it was all she could do not to cry out in agony. No position was comfortable; sitting, standing, and lying flat all hurt in one way or another.

By the time the roads finally cleared and I was able to get her to the hospital, her tumor markers had increased ten-fold and the scans revealed why: the cancer in her bones was progressing rapidly.

There was increased activity all throughout her spine and pelvis; the only good news was that Dr. Williams, at least for the moment, wasn't worried about the small spots on her neck and liver.

What he *was* worried about, however, was that the cancer had stopped responding to the chemo. It had evolved and developed some evasive mutation, allowing it to grow despite the treatment.

We were going to have to change course, and soon.

We spent that weekend at Kim and Jeff's while the pain continued to rage. Kailen propped up in a recliner surrounded by a mountain of pillows, but never could get comfortable. Her narcotic dose was off the charts, one of the highest Dr. Williams had ever prescribed, and yet the pain kept burning right through it.

She was on hydromorphone, morphine, baclofen, and gabapentin, but nothing came close to relieving the torment until we added fentanyl lollipops.

The lollipops are basically sponges infused with 200 micrograms of fentanyl. When held inside the cheek, they rapidly absorb through the buccal mucosa and provide breakthrough pain relief. They're so potent that even the direst situations rarely require more than a few a day.

Kailen was using one every two hours.

It was a long, agonizing weekend and my sense of helplessness had never been higher. I organized her medication schedule and monitored her doses, but there was nothing I could do to make anything better. I tried, but like most people in horrific pain, she wanted to be left alone.

Jeff, Jarrod, and I eventually got restless and decided to build a snowman. It gave us reason to get out of the house and momentarily took our minds off the nightmare we were living.

Looking back on it, I realize it wasn't nearly that simple. For what started off as "let's build a snowman" became "let's build the biggest snowman in the neighborhood" which then became "let's build the biggest snowman in the state" which then became "let's build the biggest snowman ever built in the history of mankind."

Over the next three days, and more than sixty man hours, we constructed an ice mountain that quite literally dwarfed the house. Kids from all over the neighborhood came by to take pictures with us, but we couldn't let them climb on our masterpiece seeing as they might fall to their actual and literal death.

It was fun and it was funny, but in retrospect it's easy to see we didn't build a snowman or an ice mountain – we built an icy Tower of Babel.

Our backbreaking effort wasn't just a testosterone-fueled display of brawny innovation; it had deep psychological and theological roots. Just like the actual Tower of Babel, we were toiling in vain, trying desperately to reach the heavens in an attempt to petition God with our plight.

Even more than that, we were protesting our own helplessness.

While Kailen suffered inside, we worked tirelessly in subzero temperatures, building a mighty frozen fortress that would melt away to nothing in a week. But the point wasn't how long it lasted, but that we built it and it existed and we existed and God cared.

It was subconscious, but by building our own version of Babel, we were choreographing a battle, and unlike the war being waged inside the house, it was a battle we could actually win.

After some debate, Kailen decided to come back with me to Ohio County on Monday. We knew things were bad and getting worse, but we stayed resilient, hoping that maybe the medication would get back on top of the pain.

It didn't.

The two-hour drive was a disaster, and that night, everything completely fell apart.

Tuesday was her 25th birthday; it was also the worst day of her life, even usurping February 4th, 2014, the day she had her childbearing capacity torn out of her with a scalpel.

I trusted Jesus Christ completely. I lived for Him, I tried to serve Him, and to the best of my ability, I lived in obedience to His commandments. And while these things are still true, I'll never understand why He took that birthday from her. Her *last* birthday.

Even if you don't.

When I walked into the bedroom that morning and looked into her eyes, something tore inside my soul, a piece of me gave way, leaving an unbridgeable chasm in the fabric of my humanity.

TeamKCT blog post (April 14th, 2015):

> *Last I posted, I had been dealing with back spasms and my right leg was very swollen with lymph fluid. A week after my last post was my 25th birthday, and unfortunately, it was one of the worst days of my life.*

> *I woke up a little after midnight on my birthday morning because my bed was soaked after I had battled some pretty severe hot flashes. (Because of these hot flashes, Bryan was sleeping in a different bed at the time so I could better regulate my body temperature and hopefully not have as many flashes.)*

> *So, I got up, changed clothes, changed my sheets, and tried to go back to sleep. However, a few hours later, I woke up once again to damp clothes and a damp bed. This time, I was so fed up that I decided to get up and take a shower before trying to go back to bed again.*

> *At this point, it's 3 o'clock the morning of my birthday and I am in the shower bawling because I could already tell what kind of day was ahead of me.*

> *After I showered, I tried to go back to sleep but never could. Instead, I stayed awake, threw*

up several times, and continued to cry as the pain all throughout my body became more and more intense. I stayed in bed until everyone else started getting up and that's when Bryan came into my room to see me. As soon as he saw my face, he knew what kind of night I had battled and he too knew what kind of day lay ahead.

You've heard the saying, "cancer is no discerner of persons." Well, it's also true that cancer doesn't care whether it's your birthday. And this past birthday, I learned the truth of that saying all too well.

I guess I should also mention that my birthday fell during the time when Bryan was on rotation in Madisonville, so we were staying at his parents' house for six weeks. Because of that, I was extra excited for my birthday because that meant my family was coming from Oldham County and we were all going to be together to celebrate.

My family did end up coming to celebrate with me, we had all my favorite foods to eat, and I was blessed with some beautiful presents, but I don't remember hardly any of it. By the evening, I was in so much pain and on so much medicine, I was wiped out and everything became a blur.

Sadly, I do remember the worst part of my birthday though. By the end of the celebration, Bryan and I just looked at each other because we knew I wasn't going to be in Ohio County much longer. We knew I needed to pack my bags

Even if you don't.

and get back to Louisville. And we knew I needed to get to the doctor. So that's what I did.

I had to leave my husband on the night of my birthday, get in a car, and make one of the most painful 2-hour drives of my life.

However, I did make it! I made it back to my parents' house, had a fitful night's sleep, and went to the hospital the next morning. (P.S. We BARELY made it to the hospital. We ran into major traffic, my dad got out of the car to tell a semi driver to radio ahead so everyone would let us through, my nose started bleeding all over my new shirt, we drove about 6 miles on the rumble strip, and THEN we finally made it to the hospital just before all my medicine started to wear off.)

But we did make it. I stayed in the hospital for about 5 days and was then released to go home and start taking chemo pills.

She said seven words when I walked into the room that morning. They were the seven words that finally broke me irreparably, and I still hear them every single day:

"All I wanted was a *bird-day breffust.*"

The "chemo pills" Kailen referred to were a drug called Afinitor.

It was our second attempt at oral chemotherapy, and while Afinitor had nowhere near the potency of the intravenous chemo, its utility was derived from the simple fact that it was different. It attacked the cancer with a unique pharmacologic mechanism, which Dr. Williams hoped would stifle the cancer's evasiveness. But even if it worked, it would only be a matter of time before the cancer mutated again and we'd be right back at square one.

It *did* work, though. As a matter of fact, it worked with exceptional efficiency.

Within a few weeks, Kailen's tumor markers were cut in half and still falling. The pain in her back and hips was starting to fade, and though it never fully went away, she jumped right back into her Tone It Up regimen. She had a broken bone in each hip and was running and doing calisthenics twice a day – two-a-days on two broken hips, no big deal.

Her rapid improvement was nothing short of miraculous – from deathbed to workout in less than a month – but it felt eerily familiar. We claimed it as our miracle, as God's ultimate and complete healing of Kailen's body, but neither of us could deny the foreboding sense of apocalypse stirring deep inside us.

Though Kailen never stopped believing that God was going to heal her, we knew our time was running out.

So, we lived.

We went to Indianapolis for the Final Four and

watched Kentucky *almost* complete a perfect basketball season; we watched fireworks at Thunder Over Louisville and I held her tight against me as a cacophony of explosions filled the cool night air; we saw Kenny Chesney and Jake Owen perform at the YUM Center; and, thanks to an anonymous benefactor, we went to Daytona Beach at the end of April.

The trip was everything we hoped it would be, a relaxing getaway and time in the sun. We spent lazy days on the beach and long evenings driving along the coast in the convertible I rented from the airport. We found a local diner down the street where we ate pancakes and sipped coffee, and there was a Dairy Queen across from the hotel where we got our daily helping of guilt-free ice cream. We walked the beach at dawn with free hotel coffee, then again at dusk with gas station beer.

The moments were serene, muted but roaring, and I fought with all I had to memorize every last one of them.

On the day we left, we stood at the water's edge for a long time. Kailen collected sand in a peanut jar, a Combs family tradition, and I just stepped back, watching her.

Eventually she sat the jar aside and waded ankle-deep into the ocean. She was facing away from me, her hands on her hips, staring out at the endless stretch of water, but I imagine her eyes were closed. I imagine she was listening to the waves crash, feeling the power of the ebbing tide beneath her feet. I imagine she was quietly appreciating the creative splendor of her

Creator's creation, blissfully lost in the juxtaposition of light and time and their perpetual fading. And I imagine she was thinking of heaven.

I imagine, but I'll never know for sure.

It was the last time she would ever see the ocean. And as we drove away, I think we both knew it.

♥ ♥ ♥

A week after we got back from Daytona, we won a great victory: I graduated from pharmacy school.

It was a battle almost five years in the making, a fight that had consumed the entirety of my and Kailen's marriage. It took enormous perseverance and required immense personal sacrifice, from both of us. So much so, I've often wondered why we did it.

In a recent conversation with Jeff and Kim, Jeff reminded me why we stuck it out, why we sacrificed such copious amounts of precious time. He said, "You staying in pharmacy school allowed Kailen to keep dreaming. If you had quit, cancer would have won. But you didn't. You kept fighting, no matter the obstacle, and she fed off your resiliency. Your sacrifice gave her reason to dream and hope, which, in my opinion, kept her alive."

Cancer stole so much of our future, but despite its best efforts, it never took pharmacy. If I'm being honest, I don't even really like pharmacy all that much. I pursued it as a career because one of my greatest aspirations in life is to provide for my family. My true passion is writing, and seeing as most writers struggle to even feed themselves, I figured I better have a lucrative day job.

Kailen knew all this; she knew I had no particular affection for the profession of pharmacy, but she also knew I was doing it for *her*. I was doing it for us and our family. Pharmacy school and its many trials were an intentional investment in our future, so if I had given up, if I had allowed the sleepless nights or the agonizing hours of study or the weeks away from my ailing wife to keep me from finishing, it would have been like I was giving up on our future.

Quitting school would have been tantamount with telling Kailen: "Look, you're dying and we have no future, so let's just spend as much time together as we can."

I refused to do that, and I think Jeff's right – by fighting my fight, I gave Kailen reason to keep fighting hers.

The graduation ceremony was deeply emotional. My parents cried, my Mamaw cried, Kim and Jeff cried, and Kailen full-on wept through the whole thing. The battle had taken a heavy toll, so seeing me walk across the stage to accept my diploma was a transcendent experience for both of us, a much-needed phenotypic display of God's faithfulness.

There was a long procession and a big crowd, but when I finally found Kailen outside the building, she ran to me, tears still streaming down her face. She jumped into my arms and I squeezed her as tightly as I could before wrapping one arm around her waist, leaning her back, and kissing her firmly on the cheek.

Either mom or Kim, or more likely both, snapped a picture of the moment. When they showed it to me, I was struck by how similar it looked to *V-J Day in Times Square,* the famous photograph of a sailor kissing a woman in a white dress to celebrate the end of World War II.

Even if you don't.

The symbolism is obvious, but it was that realization that helped me understand the real reason I became a pharmacist: just like the icy Tower of Babel, pharmacy school gave us a battle we could win.

From the very first moment we found out Kailen had cancer, we had no chance. The prognosis was never anything but terminal; no matter how hard we fought or how many treatment modalities we employed, we were going to lose the war and she was going to die.

But pharmacy school gave us a chance. It embodied all our hopes and dreams, it symbolized our future, and together, we fought for it. And together, we won.

That fateful image – me in my cap and gown, her in a purple dress – now serves as an iconic reminder of the victory we achieved, of the life we lived.

Our fight was a testament to the undying love we had for one another, and as Kailen always said, to the faithfulness of our God.

TeamKCT blog post (May 23rd, 2015):

> *Pharmacy school has been a part of our lives from the very beginning. We met in November 2009, and at that point, he was applying to the University of Kentucky College of Pharmacy, preparing for the PCAT, taking the PCAT, waiting for results, getting accepted, and then had his interview...*
>
> *We were married in December of 2010; afterwards, Bryan finished his last semester of*

undergrad at UK in the spring of 2011, then pharmacy school began the following August, just 8 months into our marriage.

Our lives became an endless cycle of classes, homework, labs, studying for blocks, locking in for blocks, taking block exams, recovering from block exams for a day or two, and then the cycle would begin all over again! It. Was. Crazy.

But Bryan never let up, he studied harder than most, he never let it get him down, and he pushed through the first year. And you know what? Our God was ever faithful.

Then, in September of 2012, in the beginning of Bryan's second year of pharmacy school, cancer hit. Suddenly, our lives became an endless cycle of classes, homework, labs, getting me to chemo, getting me back from chemo, Bryan tending to my needs when I was too sick to help him, studying for blocks, having any imaging or medical testing I needed, locking in for blocks, surgery after surgery, taking block exams, recovery from blocks being spent at the hospital, and then...the cycle would start all over again.

However, Bryan never let up, he studied harder than most, he studied in hospital waiting rooms, he was always there to be my strength when I had none, he fought every day to not let it get him down, and he pushed through his second year of pharmacy school. And our God was ever faithful.

Even if you don't.

After the end of the second year, we had a relatively normal summer. We got to go on our first vacation just the two of us, I was getting stronger and stronger, my prognosis was trending upwards, and we had a brief break from the endless cycle. But our vacation was bittersweet. We had a great time, but we knew what we were coming home to. We were coming home to the beginnings of another crazy cycle, and this time, it was going to be kicked off by me having a mastectomy, then an extensive recovery, and we still had no idea if the cancer was gone for sure. But the semester still started, ready or not, and we really didn't feel ready.

However, Bryan never let up, he studied harder than most, he walked with me through mastectomy and then ovary removal in the second semester, we recovered, we walked through radiation, we recovered again, he never neglected his studies, he fought to never let it get him down, and finally, we had pushed through the third year of pharmacy school. And our God was ever faithful.

Immediately after third year, we began a full year of rotations. We moved to Bryan's parents for 6 weeks, we moved back, he worked his two rotations over the summer, and then, in September of 2014, my hips started to hurt. Suddenly I could barely stand, much less walk, and Bryan had to end his rotation, thus sacrificing his actual vacation block so he could be with me at the hospital. I was hospitalized for a while, the cancer had spread quite a bit, I underwent immediate radiation, I got out of the hospital, and then we were somehow faced with chemo again.

Still, Bryan never let up, he held my hand through everything, we got tattoos and his said, "Stay in the Fight," which is exactly what he always did. We had a big haircutting party where I cut my hair short for the second time, countless friends cut/shaved their hair off, TeamKCT was battle-ready more than ever, and we were prepared to begin the second big go-round of our fight.

Bryan resumed his next rotation, we moved for the first time so we could be closer to doctors, I went to chemo every week, I lost all my hair again, I lost all my energy, and I was trapped at home. But Bryan was with me the whole time and...our God was ever faithful.

At this point, it was the beginning of 2015, the year we had been waiting for our entire marriage. We just had to get through a few more months. Chemo would soon be over for me, Bryan would graduate, and we would be free to live decently normal adult lives.

But then, my birthday came and if you have been following the blog, you know what a hellacious day that was for us. Suddenly we were right back in the scare of cancer spreading. I had to begin a new chemo, my leg was swollen with lymph fluid to three times its normal size due to radiation-damaged lymph

Even if you don't.

nodes, and those measly few months until graduation seemed like forever.

I can't lie, things were looking pretty bleak at that point.

But that's when God stepped in yet again.

He gave us a renewed peace, joy, and sense of purpose. Bryan worked his butt off in his last few rotations, he was blessed with the best preceptors, some of TeamKCT sent us on a beyond-needed vacation, one of his rotations led to him getting a pharmacist position with the wonderful company of Kroger, and in the blink of an eye, it was time for Bryan to walk across that stage.

So, if you look back and see the graduation pictures where I was absolutely bawling, you will understand some of the emotion behind those tears.

I wasn't simply watching my husband walk across a stage and graduate from pharmacy school. No no no, I was watching a son of the most-high God, a timeworn soldier, a man who NEVER quit, a man who had walked with God so intimately, a man who absolutely refused to be beaten, a man who ALWAYS stayed in the fight, and I was watching MY man finally survive when an enemy had tried so desperately to kill our success.

The enemy tried every trick in the book, but

guess what?

In the end, Bryan walked across that stage, accepted the diploma he had earned, and I could not have been prouder of my husband.

And still, our God was ever faithful!

After graduation, Kailen's healing miracle continued gaining momentum. She was still taking the oral chemo, Afinitor, along with an oral hormone suppressant and her usual armamentarium of pain medication. She was neither disease-free nor symptom-free, but she was getting better every day.

She immersed herself in the TIU Bikini Series, and as she strengthened her emaciated musculature, the pain started to go away. The fractures in her hips were almost completely healed and as she strengthened her core, the added stability helped attenuate the back pain. Meanwhile, the crippling lymphedema in her right leg was completely gone.

In February she could barely walk, even with the assistance of a cane; by the middle of May, she was running three miles a day.

Suddenly, the healing we'd thought was temporary, the miracle we'd thought was a mirage, was starting to feel like the real thing. And people were starting to notice.

The popularity of Kailen's blog was growing

exponentially. With every post, she was garnering tens of thousands of views from all over the world. She kept a tally on her phone of all the countries that had read the blog, and by the summer of 2015, that number had reached fifty-four. *Fifty-four* nations, from Canada and Mexico to Russia and China, to Israel, to Greece, to England and France, to Saudi Arabia, to India, to Australia and Indonesia, to South Africa, to Spain, to Greenland and Iceland.

Kailen's story had quite literally reached every corner of the world.

But she wasn't stopping there.

She began accepting a greater number of speaking engagements. Everyone wanted to know about the twenty-five-year-old that had stared stage IV cancer in the face and lived to tell the tale. But more than that, they wanted some of her magic. They wanted their congregation, or their staff, or their student body, to experience her, to somehow touch the intangible part of her that kept her smiling and laughing and pressing on with such incomparable courage.

When she announced she was going to write a book, the excitement resonated through her blog viewers, her friends and family, and her ever-growing list of admirers.

The anticipation was already high, but something happened in June that brought it to a fever pitch:

Kailen won the 2015 Tone It Up Bikini Series Grand Prize.

The Tone It Up community gave Kailen purpose when everything else had been taken away. This is her Bikini Series submission letter, and in it, you can see just how much TIU meant to her (taken from TeamKCT blog post, June 23rd, 2015):

Tone It Up and the Bikini Series changed my life this year by helping to give me back a life worth living. I battled Crohn's Disease for over a decade and it severely depleted my quality of life. I was a few months away from having my colon removed and being disease-free when, in 2012, at the age of 22, I was diagnosed with stage IV breast cancer. Needless to say, my fitness life was drastically altered.

That diagnosis happened three years ago. Since then I've been through chemo twice, radiation twice, and had countless surgeries. Some days all I want to do is stay in bed, and admittedly, some days I do! But one day I discovered TIU and the Bikini Series.

After all my treatments, I was very weak. And at the beginning of the series, I could barely walk. Some of my lymph nodes were greatly damaged from radiation and my leg was swollen with 15 pounds of lymph fluid. Still, I was able to adapt TIU exercises to my level of fitness and build strength from there. I started slowly but it wasn't long before I started to see progress. Between seeing results, loving the lifestyle of the nutrition plan, and discovering the power of my sisters in the TIU community, I was EXTREMELY motivated to press on!

Even if you don't.

This series I lost 15 pounds of lymph fluid, 10 pounds of fat, and 2.5 inches off my waist. I increased my flexibility and I ultimately gained my life back. I can now run when I could barely walk, lift when I could barely stand, and I am living when I thought my life as I knew it was over. Thank you, Karena and Katrina, for giving me my life back!

It was the whole "indomitable fervor" thing again. Kailen had one breast, no ovaries, no colon, two broken hips, and a bag of crap taped to her stomach, and she went and won a national fitness competition.

She was boldly unbroken, unstoppable in her pursuit of life even in the face of death.

When Tone It Up interviewed Kailen on their website, they asked her how she was able to overcome such dramatic setbacks. Kailen wrote these words to her fellow sisters in the TIU community:

"I have always been an active person, but between battling Crohn's disease for over a decade, getting diagnosed with cancer, going through chemotherapy, having my colon removed, having one breast removed, doing radiation, having my ovaries removed, having the cancer spread all over again, going through chemotherapy again, radiation again, having the cancer spread all over again, and now being on a more mild, oral chemotherapy...I've had a lot to overcome.

But rather than let each trial bring me further and further down, I chose to let it fuel me to press on and overcome the impossible."

For Kailen, overcoming the impossible was part of her daily routine. Winning the Bikini Series was a very public example, but Kailen's true magic was hidden in the mundanities of life, like waking up with a smile, sipping coffee, reading a book, or walking the dogs at sunset. No matter what she endured physically, her spiritual sense of wonder held true. Every moment, even the most ordinary, possessed an inherent beauty worth fighting for, worth gazing upon with childlike awe and appreciation.

That afternoon in our living room, reading the message from Karena and Katrina informing Kailen that she had won – that was our last mountaintop moment. We had reached an emotional pinnacle, nearly convinced that the healing was real and true and permanent, and now that I was out of school, we had finally arrived in that elusive land of milk and honey called Normalcy.

Our life, it seemed, was about to begin.

But fate said otherwise.

Less than twenty-four hours later, on June 21st, 2015, Father's Day, I was working at a pharmacy in Danville when Dr. Williams sent me the text that set the stage for the beginning of the end.

It said, simply: *We need to talk.*

Part Four

The Gloaming

"A man can be destroyed but not defeated."

-Ernest Hemingway, *The Old Man and the Sea*

Those last few months were lived in a perpetual dusk. The sun no longer shone brightly, but rather painted the world in a somber, pale orange, as though it were perched tenuously upon the horizon and couldn't decide whether to rise or set.

Life was now a monochromatic limbo.

The Bikini Series Grand Prize was an all-expenses paid trip to an exclusive resort in Playa del Carmen,

Mexico. It was the trip of a lifetime; unfortunately, we didn't have enough lifetime left to enjoy it.

We never went to Mexico. We never went anywhere ever again.

Dr. Williams "needed to talk" because the cancer had gone to Kailen's liver. He had always told us that malignancy contained to the bone is manageable, and with diligent treatment, could be kept relatively static for many years, possibly even decades. But that was no longer our situation.

The most recent scans had revealed the liver lesion, and in so doing, irrevocably altered Kailen's prognosis. Now that there was soft tissue involvement, especially in a critical organ like the liver, maintaining stable disease over any significant period of time would be almost impossible.

In short, the cancer was in a sprint to the finish line.

On July 1st, Kailen underwent a procedure called chemoembolization. It was a clever technique that sought to abolish the lesion via two different mechanisms: first, they threaded a catheter through an artery in Kailen's leg and ran it all the way into her abdomen, near the site of the lesion. Once there, they released chemo-soaked beads directly onto the surface of her liver. This was meant to kill the cancer through direct contact with chemotherapy.

After the beads were released, the doctor cauterized the artery through which he accessed the liver, resulting in a complete loss of blood supply, making it impossible for the cancer to survive. The oxygen deprivation would also kill the healthy liver tissue, but the hope was that the healthy tissue would regenerate and the malignancy wouldn't.

The procedure was outpatient and purportedly simple. It took about an hour. When it was done, the doctor told us things had gone as well as possible and there had been no unforeseen complications.

What he didn't tell us, however, was that the surgery itself was the easy part.

The artery the doctor had used to insert the catheter was on the inside of Kailen's left thigh, and while the risk was relatively low, the fact that Kailen was on blood thinners increased her odds of post-surgical bleeding. In order to keep that from happening, the doctor insisted she lay flat for at least six hours. Any bending or torsion at the pelvis could result in a potentially fatal arterial hemorrhage.

Easy enough, we thought. We certainly don't want a fatal hemorrhage, so we'll lie here for a few hours, watch some TV, take a nap, then get out of here. Right?

Wrong.

They were six of the worst hours of my life. Lying flat was one of the absolute worst postures for Kailen, and within twenty minutes her hips and back were roaring with pain. She toughed it out at first, gritting her teeth and telling me she was okay, swallowing her tears. But pain eventually breaks everyone.

By the hour mark, she was screaming.

She was writhing and thrashing and crying, begging me to let her sit up, begging me to take away the pain. But as usual, I was helpless. Every part of my human spirit was already broken, so I maintained my equanimity and held my hands on her shoulders, resisting her desperate convulsions and pressing her firmly against the bed.

My wife was dying; I had known it for almost three years. I was universally impotent, powerless to do anything but love her with everything I had left. And in those wicked hours following the chemoembolization, I pressed her shoulders and kissed away her tears and held the bucket when she vomited.

She was dying and I couldn't stop it, but she wasn't going to bleed out that day. *That* I could stop.

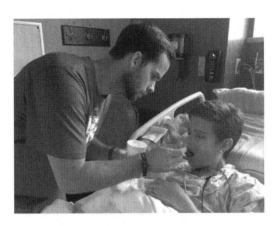

With the help of several doses of pain medication, we survived the six hours. We then spent the night at Norton Audubon, one of the few hospitals in the greater Louisville area we hadn't slept in. And despite the overnight stay, we still haven't slept at Norton Audubon. Because, in point of fact, we didn't sleep.

Kailen tossed and turned in agony while I argued with the nurses in an attempt to get her more medication. Then, at dawn, I left to go to work and Kim came to stay with her until she was discharged later that day.

Kailen had made a number of miraculous comebacks, and as I left the hospital that morning to drive back to Frankfort, I was praying and believing it would happen again.

Somehow, some way, I'd wake up in a few days and find her in the living room doing a Tone It Up workout. She'll bounce back because that's what she always does. God would make a way where there seemed to be no way; this was just another obstacle in our path to healing, another divine test to pass. We'd been in this hole before, deeper even, and had always climbed out. We would simply have to do it again.

But not this time. This was different.

After the chemoembolization, Kailen was never the same. She never got better. She felt horrible almost all the time, battled perpetual pain and exhaustion, and could barely get out of bed. She was weak and getting weaker, so thin you could see the gentle curvature of her bones.

A few nights later I was awoken by a large crashing sound. I sat straight up in bed, adrenaline pumping just as it had done with every midnight trauma before, and I shouted her name.

She wasn't in bed and she wasn't anywhere in the room. I shouted again, growing frantic. I threw off the covers and sprinted toward the only light I could see, a faint sliver emanating from beneath the bathroom door.

She's dead, I thought, my heart pounding so hard it threatened to give out. *She died right here in our house, while I was sleeping like a fool. I'm about to find my wife's corpse and the trauma will kill me. They'll find us both, entombed in our bathroom.*

When I rammed the door open, nearly removing it from its hinges, I finally saw her.

She was lying in the floor by the toilet, her neck and shoulders awkwardly pinned against the wall. She smiled weakly, but I could tell she was embarrassed.

"Oh sweetie," I said, running to her. "What happened?"

"I'm okay," she told me in a breathless whisper. "I was brushing my teeth and...I guess my hip gave out."

I ran my arms under her shoulders and lifted her gently to her feet. Beneath her arms, I could feel her ribs. There was no muscle or fat left to coat the bone, only gristle and sinew.

"I'm so sorry, K," I said, then clenched my jaw to quell my emotion. "Are you sure you're not hurt?"

She shook her head and repeated, "I'm okay."

I carried her back to bed and softly laid her on her right side, the only prone position that offered any relief from the pain. She eventually went back to sleep but I stayed awake and watched her, partly because I didn't want her to get back up without supervision, but mostly because I didn't want to waste a single moment in her presence.

As I studied the rise and fall of her tiny chest, I was reminded of something C.S. Lewis once wrote.

He said, "You don't have a soul, you *are* a soul. You have a body."

Lying there beside her as night faded to day, I knew time was running short. Her body was emaciated and decrepit, too weak even to stand. But as her body fell, her soul soared. Her skeleton, that earthly carbon capsule she inhabited, was inching ever closer to the grave, but all the while her soul was rising. Her body would soon be interred in the dirt, but she, Kailen, the woman I loved, with whom I had become one, in her truest essence, was homeward bound.

I wanted to cry but couldn't, so I rolled over and rubbed her back until I fell asleep.

A few days after the fall, at an appointment with Dr. Williams, he explained to us why Kailen had been feeling so terrible. He pointed at an image on his computer screen.

"Do you know what that is?" he asked.

Kailen and I both shook our heads that we didn't.

"That's your liver. The lighter area is live tissue, but the space that's in shadow was all killed by the embolization. No wonder you haven't been yourself."

Almost a third of Kailen's liver had been killed by the procedure. The news was actually positive, considering the lesion was also dead, but a 30% loss of hepatic function would make anyone feel like death warmed over.

Even still, we clung to the good news. The embolization had been effective and there was no longer any visible cancer anywhere in her visceral organs. We walked out of the appointment with grateful and hopeful hearts – grateful for any victory over this terrible disease, and hopeful that Kailen would slowly start feeling better as her liver recovered.

But once again, she didn't get better.

One of our friends got married the following week and Kailen, who loved weddings, almost didn't attend. The pain in her hips and spine had returned unabridged and her body was so weak she could only walk with the assistance of a cane.

It was a beautiful wedding on a warm summer day; the ceremony was conducted at a botanical garden and the trees and flowers bloomed all around us in extravagant and mesmerizing color. It should have been one of those youthful moments you preserve in scrapbooks and show your kids someday. And I realized, even then, that for most of our friends that's exactly the kind of day it was.

But our light was fading, and the color along with it.

We were once again surrounded by those that loved us but didn't know us, and there is no greater loneliness than being loved but unknown.

The pain and weakness continued to worsen until one day in late July, Kailen told me about a new symptom.

"I feel pressure and tingling in my head," she told me. "It's like someone is tickling it from the inside, then squeezing my brain like a stress ball."

We knew what it could be and immediately began praying against it. I didn't show it, especially not to her, but I was incredibly scared. I was scared that this horrible disease had invaded my wife's brain, and that now, she would die before she was really dead.

Her sweet personality, her unwavering quirkiness, her brilliance and humor – what if the cancer stole it? What if she couldn't speak and I never got to hear her voice again? Or her heart-melting giggle? Or the high-pitched squeal she employed when she was pretending to be mad at me?

Somehow, the thought of her dying and being truly gone was easier to accept; it fit into the grief template I had been constructing for years. But this, this was something different.

Dr. Williams was very concerned, as we knew he would be. He ordered a brain MRI for the next day. The imaging appointment required us to make another trip to Norton Audubon, and just like before, our stay was less than pleasant.

We were there for almost three hours as they tried and failed to find a vein in Kailen's arms. To their credit, Kailen's veins were tiny and had a tendency to roll when prodded, but after three hours of needle sticks, sitting in a cold room coping with agonizing bone pain, I told the nurse enough was enough. They would just have to do the MRI without contrast because I wasn't making my wife endure this any longer.

So, they did. And two days later, on July 24th, we got the results.

They were negative. There was no evidence of cancer anywhere in Kailen's brain or skull.

Everyone rejoiced and breathed an enormous sigh of relief. Everyone except me. I *did* thank God for the good news, but inwardly I couldn't deny my intuition. The lack of IV contrast basically made the MRI useless. As much as I wanted the results to be true, I knew they were invalid.

When Dr. Williams realized no contrast had been used, he ordered a repeat scan. It was like winning the lottery then having someone tell you there was a mistake, that the money actually belonged to someone else. Kailen hobbled back into the hospital, leaning on her cane, got prodded again, endured another scan while the cancerous fire raged inside her spine, and was so exhausted by the time she got home I'm not sure she even cared about the results.

That was a feeling that characterized that whole summer: we were tired, so *very* tired, the kind of fatigue that pervades the soul and impacts one's will to live.

The War had worn us down more than we realized, and as we yet again waited for our fate to be decided by a machine, a sense of spiritual apathy sought to consume us.

Praying became difficult; asking God for healing felt like talking to the wall. Hope was the dagger that had severed my heart and I wanted so desperately to give up, to quit begging for healing I no longer believed in from a God I wasn't sure was even listening.

But I asked anyway. Hundreds of times a day.

And every night I knelt beside our bed, my knees aching against the hardwood floor, and led Kailen in prayer. I placed my hands on her body and asked God to be God, to intervene on our behalf. I'm certain He heard me, but He chose otherwise.

I got the text two days later.

I was working at a pharmacy in Frankfort. It was mid-morning, sometime around 10:00 or 10:30. The air outside was muggy and thick, wrought with the hot moisture of late July. I felt my phone buzz inside my white coat but was too busy to look at it right away.

It was after 11:00 when I finally checked it and saw

who it was from.

Dr. Patrick Williams: *Call me.*

I ran to the back and dialed his number. He answered on the third ring and the mere sound of his voice confirmed my darkest fears. The cancer had coiled itself into the meningeal layer surrounding Kailen's brain. The prognosis was dire and our options were limited.

The sun, resting tenuously on the horizon, had decided to set.

♥ ♥ ♥

In our odyssey of pain, next came the lumbar punctures.

Kailen laid flat on her stomach, which hurt quite a lot, while a doctor inserted a needle into her spinal canal, which hurt quite a lot *more*. The purpose of the procedure was to take a sample of cerebrospinal fluid (CSF) in an attempt to characterize the nature of the cancer in Kailen's meninges. They also injected methotrexate, a chemotherapeutic agent, directly into the canal in hopes that the flow of CSF would transport the drug up the spine and into the brain.

Despite being really painful, the lumbar punctures were an outpatient procedure. We were in and out in less than two hours.

After eating lunch in Louisville, we drove back to Frankfort and tried desperately to focus our minds on other things. I did yard work while Kailen knitted and watched TV. It was as though the reality of our situation was so obvious it would have been redundant to talk about it. So, we didn't.

As a general principle, we chose to live while we could. Death was coming, and with it a cosmic separation, which led us to the unspoken conclusion that sitting and talking about death was a waste of time. We weren't so foolish and naïve as to believe we could ignore it, but dwelling on it gave it power it didn't deserve.

Though Kailen had terminal cancer, she was technically no closer to death than me or anyone else; the breadth of a single heartbeat is all that separates any of us from our eternal fate.

In other words, death isn't special or unique. But life is. And we decided to treat it as such.

Over the next few days, the bone pain reached an unprecedented level. Dr. Williams and I continuously adjusted Kailen's medication, eventually reaching a dose that would have killed her three months earlier, but now the pain burned through it as if it were a placebo.

Outside of the thirty-minute period following a fentanyl lollipop, there was no relief. The agony was untenable.

Our last day at home, August 1st, 2015, makes a strong case for the worst day of our lives, right up there with ovary removal and Kailen's 25th birthday.

As I said, she was now in constant, impregnable pain. But despite all she had been through, Kailen rarely verbalized her discomfort. If she was hurting moderately, there was absolutely no way to tell; if she was hurting badly, she simply got quiet; if she was hurting really badly, she would sometimes moan or close her eyes.

But on August 1st, everything changed.

She was screaming and crying, a tortured guttural sound coming from her throat. I held her and kissed her and prayed, and it was all just as futile as the medicine.

Eventually, I ran a few inches of warm water in the bathtub and she laid in it. The warmth seemed to help some, but looking back I suspect she was feigning relief just to make me feel better. Either way, it didn't last long.

I sat on the toilet and stared blankly at the shower curtain. She'd had me close the curtain and the bathroom door because she was incredibly cold and beginning to shiver, which scared me. I knew we were about to head to the hospital; oral pain medication was now useless, no matter how high the dose. If I didn't get her access to IV narcotics within a few hours, she was going to die.

I was about to start the process of packing everything up when she said something that stopped me cold.

"Why doesn't God just let me die?" she shouted. "Please, just let me die!"

I couldn't see her because of the curtain, and anytime I pulled it back, she quickly reprimanded me. So I just knelt down on the floor outside the tub.

"I'm here with you, sweetie," I assured her. "I'm right here. You aren't alone."

It was the best I had. What do you say to your wife when she asks a completely legitimate question to which you don't have a legitimate answer? As desperately as I wanted her to live, to grow old with me, to get her miracle, I knew it wasn't coming. And if it wasn't coming, if death was inevitable, why would God allow such nihilistic suffering?

If there's anything worse than losing your spouse, it's watching your spouse beg for a death that just won't come.

After I composed myself, I stepped out of the bathroom and called Kim. She and Jeff then contacted Dr. Williams and the wonderful staff at Norton Suburban immediately got a room ready for us. We arrived at the hospital two hours later and I rolled Kailen gently down the hallway in a wheelchair.

The elevator carried us up to the fifth floor – the *cancer* floor – and as Jeff and I went back to the car to carry everything in, the nurses quickly got an IV started.

It took several hours for the pain to abate, but when it did, Kailen finally fell into a deep, much-needed sleep. Once again, I didn't rest. I couldn't.

I just sat by the bed and prayed to God she would wake up one more time.

I spent those hot August hospital mornings walking and praying. My first stop was the Starbucks on the first floor, where I picked up the same order every day and carried it back to the room. Kailen and I sipped our coffee together while she watched Chip and Joanna Gaines on HGTV, then we'd walk out onto the rooftop terrace in the center of the fifth floor.

The terrace was meant to be a place of solitude and refuge; there was a smattering of tables and benches, surrounded by well-tended landscaping. Flowers of every color bloomed in large pots, while burgundy Japanese maples grew along the walkway. The fifth floor was the top floor, so even though you could hear the hum of the city below, all you could see was the sky.

We had to be back to the room by around 11, which was when patient transport came to take Kailen down to radiation. It was completely palliative and Dr. Williams had ordered it almost immediately upon admission. The radiation, along with an incremental increase in her narcotic dosage, had finally overpowered the pain.

Unfortunately, now we had a big decision to make. Dr. Williams had done extensive research on how to proceed, including consulting some of the world's top specialists. There were options available, but none were promising.

There was a clinical trial about to start that would be testing the efficacy of an experimental drug against brain cancer. We *hated* that option – the words 'trial' and 'experimental' don't exactly imbue a sense of confidence – but Kailen's previous exposure to multiple forms of chemotherapy limited our choices.

At this point, the cancer was too smart to respond to anything but a massive dose of something really potent. We had been fighting with heavy artillery for a long time, but now we needed a bomb. We needed a chemotherapeutic that would come in and decimate everything. The catch, of course, was that such an agent would also decimate Kailen. And in her current state, it was unlikely she would survive the trauma.

We eventually decided to give the clinical trial a shot. But within a matter of days, we got a call informing us that Kailen was not a good candidate for the study. They were looking to investigate primary site brain cancers, not metastases.

Thus, we were left with our handful of bombs.

Dr. Williams listed off two or three agents with therapeutic potential, all of which I remembered from class and inwardly cringed at the thought of, and there was also the option of doing aggressive head and neck radiation.

Basically, we were death row inmates being given the option of how we wanted to die: slowly and honorably, or quickly and with some shred of dignity.

We didn't decide right away. We prayed and focused

our efforts on trying to survive one day at a time. I was still working full-time, which meant I slept at the hospital every night and made the commute back and forth to Frankfort. The lack of sleep didn't really bother me – I had years of practice – but the time away from Kailen certainly did. I checked my phone compulsively throughout the day, ever-fearful of the call finally confirming she was truly gone.

Two weeks passed. We still hadn't made a decision regarding our next step, but we had tried to take Kailen home once.

The rationale was simple: if these were her final days, they should be lived at home, not in the hospital. Plus, just about any treatment, including radiation, could be initiated on an outpatient basis. It made enough sense.

The only problem was the pain.

Within six hours of stopping the IV narcotics, Kailen could barely breathe. We were back in our hospital room in less than twenty-four hours.

Then, on August 15th, things took a very scary turn. Kailen became non-responsive. For almost two days, she sunk into what Dr. Williams called a pseudo-coma. She didn't eat, she didn't drink, and she didn't speak. In fact, she barely moved.

She was gone; I knew it this time. I would never see her blue irises ever again.

It's tough to describe what that realization did to me.

You can't break what's already broken, so I didn't exactly collapse. I just sort of glazed over and went quiet, as though whatever humanity I had left had been put on eternal mute.

But the hardest part, the part I feel guilty about, is the part of me that *hoped* she was gone. While I yearned for her to stay with me, I couldn't shake the reality that this would be a peaceful end to a violent war. Maybe it would be as painless as dying in your sleep; maybe she wouldn't feel anything at all.

The next day was Kim's birthday and a bunch of family came to the hospital. They gathered in a waiting area down the hallway and the kids played out on the terrace.

It had been a long, difficult night. Kailen had stirred some, but not enough to give me any real hope. Just enough to confirm this was *not* a peaceful end to a violent war; if she were to die right now, it would not be like falling asleep. She was in agony.

When Dr. Williams came by on morning rounds, he increased her narcotic dose again and told me very candidly that if we didn't pick a chemo soon, it was going to be too late. The right agent at the right dose might give her another six months or more, he told me.

But it might also torture her, I thought.

And it might fail.

Worst of all, it might torture her *and* fail.

I looked at her lying there in bed and realized I would have to make the decision for her, and no matter which option I picked, I would have to live with the consequences for the rest of my life.

As dawn broke, Kailen started moaning. She tossed and turned violently in the bed, a sort of voluntary seizure. It took me a few minutes to realize the sunlight coming in through the window was the source of the discomfort. She was in such great pain that even in the faintest light reaching her eyes made the headache roar. With the help of the nursing staff, I used almost an entire roll of duct tape securing a bedsheet to the ceiling, completely blocking off the window and blacking out the room. Only then did Kailen calm down and settle back into her coma.

Dr. Williams returned around lunchtime and I decided we had to at least try something. The realization that Kailen was in pain had made the decision for me. Williams recommended two chemotherapeutics, and after trying and failing to get Kailen to sign the consent form, I signed it for her.

They infused the chemo and less than an hour later, Kailen woke up.

The first words she said were these, and this is an exact quote: "When a person is trying to die, do *not* rub them. It hurts like hell." She looked around for a moment, getting her bearings. "I need to shower. I stink."

And with that, she got out of bed and walked unassisted to the bathroom. She washed off, fixed her hair, put on make-up, and like a modern-day Lazarus, pushed her own IV pole out of the hospital room and made her way down the hallway to see her family.

When she emerged into the waiting area, I imagine the response of the crowd was not unlike Mary and Martha when they saw their brother leave the tomb.

Kim had been giving periodic updates, so when Kailen came around the corner with a smile on her face, it truly was miraculous. There were expressions of shock and surprise, tears of joy, and cries of overwhelming gratitude. But for me and Kailen, buried somewhere deep inside where no one could see, there lay something comparable to disappointment. Because after everyone else left and went home, they would go to sleep in their comfy beds and life would go on.

For us, life would not go on.

We were still in this colloquial version of hell called a hospital, still staring down the possibility of another long battle with chemo, still facing the reality of a terminal prognosis, which even our Lazarus Miracle was powerless to change.

Hours after everyone left, we went on a short walk around the unit. She could only take fifteen or twenty steps without getting winded, but we managed to complete a few laps before stopping at a bay window overlooking the parking lot. We were just chit-chatting, discussing a topic I don't remember, when my guilt overwhelmed me and I confessed.

"Part of me hoped you wouldn't wake up," I said,

looking away. "It makes me sick to even verbalize those words, but it's true. Of course I want you to live! I'd give my life for you right now if God would let me. But we've grown weary, sweetheart. The battle is long. I want you to live, but I don't want you to suffer. Not anymore."

I was ashamed of my weakness and could hardly bear to look at her. It was one of the only moments in almost three years that my equanimity had cracked.

She was silent for a while, but then she smiled. "I saw the veil today. It was thin, almost transparent, and beyond it everything was really bright. No one explained it to me but I somehow knew what it meant. I had this overwhelming desire to move toward it, and when I reached for it, everything felt right. Until I turned around and saw that you hadn't followed me. You were still standing there where I'd left you, unable to move. So, I came back to you."

"I wish I could go," I whispered.

She looked out the window and nodded. "Me too. But we're like soldiers who haven't taken their boots off in months. Our feet are sore and swollen and blistered. Maybe this coma thing was God's way of giving us a break, but now He's asking us to shove the boots back on, tear off the scabs, and open up the blisters all over again."

She shrugged. "Someday the battle will be over. It's just not today."

I had no words. All I could do was hold her hand

and try to memorize every smell, sound, and feeling. Because standing by that window with her, I had never been more tangibly in the presence of God.

The Lazarus Miracle bought us about twelve hours.

That's how long we had to wonder if maybe, just maybe, this chemo regimen could somehow be the medium through which God would orchestrate His ultimate healing. In a sense, He had already used it to save Kailen's life.

Maybe, we thought. *Maybe*, we begged. Maybe there was a tiny crack in that concrete prognosis.

But twelve hours later, Dr. Williams debunked those hopeful maybes. He told us that even though the chemo had been momentarily effective, there were really only two treatment options with any life-extending potential: high-dose methotrexate therapy or aggressive head and neck radiation.

Both options posed huge risks. The methotrexate therapy would require long inpatient stays so Kailen could be continuously monitored, but also so she could receive something called leucovorin rescue therapy.

At the risk of oversimplification, methotrexate kills cancer by inhibiting cellular ability to produce folate, a B-vitamin derivative necessary for life. As with most chemotherapies, the problem is selectivity. Methotrexate isn't able to differentiate a cancer cell from a healthy cell. The result, especially at high doses, is a complete annihilation of the patient's immune system. Leucovorin is a compound structurally similar to folate, and when injected twenty-four to forty-eight hours following methotrexate therapy, it helps replenish the folic acid needed for healthy cells to survive.

The idea is that methotrexate kills the cancer cells and then leucovorin is given just in time to rescue the healthy ones. This is the ideal situation, which in the world of cancer therapy, doesn't actually exist.

In Kailen's deteriorated condition, the methotrexate could easily kill her. Not to mention, with her life expectancy quickly dwindling, there was always the chance that methotrexate would simply be a nuisance.

Was an extra month or two really worth it if she had to live it bald, unable to swallow, with mouth sores, and diarrhea, and nerve damage?

Then there was the radiation option. Dr. Williams scheduled a consult for us to discuss the decision with a radiation oncologist, but in the meantime, he made it clear it would not be pleasant. She would likely lose her hair permanently, the dose would be higher than anything she'd previously had and thus the burns would be more severe, but worst of all was the potential for irreparable brain damage. It was entirely possible that Kailen could lose her ability to speak.

Our third and final option was doing nothing.

Dr. Williams didn't rush us or try to sway us one way or the other. He was anxious and clearly wanted to proceed with treatment, but he walked us through the process like a loving parent, not a doctor.

He prayed with us almost every day, on his knees, in a thousand-dollar suit, on a dirty hospital floor. I could live the rest of my life and never meet another person quite like The Little General. And in fact, I expect to.

While we were busy making our decision, the farewell visits started pouring in. Friends we hadn't seen or heard from in a while began showing up unannounced, bringing coffee and flowers and handwritten notes of encouragement.

It was sincerely appreciated. But I admit, in many cases, the encounters left a bitter taste in my mouth. Because even though our friends are wonderful people, and frankly, wonderful *friends,* they were young and had no idea how to handle a stage IV cancer diagnosis. As a result, they weren't there for us the way we had hoped they would be.

Kailen and I spent a lot of time feeling lonely and confused.

To be clear, though you've probably noticed one of the main sub-themes of this story is my and Kailen's perception of abandonment during our cancer battle, especially from our friends, the key word contained therein is *perception.*

Though I've intentionally illustrated this concept in the narrative, primarily for the benefit of other young widows and widowers who will invariably contend with the same perceptions, please understand that Kailen and I had a remarkable support system. Our friends were, and are, amazing people. There are dozens of stories of their love and faithfulness I could have included.

So, as you continue reading, please realize my focus is on how Kailen and I *felt*, not on the actual shortcomings of our friends. Kailen and I were extremely grateful for each and every act of support we ever received, and I still am to this day. Without the love of our friends, we couldn't have fought as we did.

Finally, if you're enduring great hardship, let me encourage you to extend unyielding empathy and grace to your loved ones. Realize they're likely grieving too, and in almost every case, are doing the best they can.

I know our friends supported us far more than I remember – *pain powerfully skews perspective* – but in light of our feelings of abandonment, those farewell visits seemed somewhat unsubstantiated.

A notable exception was Alex Weires. During that last hospital stay, she either came or offered to come every single day.

She didn't often bring gifts and she never announced her good deeds, but she *sat* with us. She *talked* to us. She *hugged* us. She made us feel human. She made Kailen feel loved and understood. She made me feel appreciated.

She did what Job's friends did for him when he had lost everything and everyone – she practiced the Ministry of Presence, and she did it faithfully.

People often tell me that Kailen lived longer because

of the way I loved her. If that's true, and I sure hope it is, then Alex deserves credit, too.

♥ ♥ ♥

Toward the end of August, Kailen's brother Jarrod had a successful post-colectomy reversal. He, like Kailen, had been diagnosed with Crohn's disease. But instead of enduring the painstaking litany of steroids and immunosuppressants, Jarrod had decided to go ahead and have his colon removed.

That procedure had taken place on June 18th. He had his reversal surgery on August 24th, and two days later was walking around good as new, Crohn's-free.

Kailen and I were obviously very excited for him. It was exactly what we had prayed for, complete healing with no complications. But it also turned Jarrod into a walking talking reminder of what-could-have-been.

What if we hadn't tried Remicade? Would Kailen be up walking around instead of lying in this bed, preparing to die at age 25? Maybe she'd be a pharmacist. Maybe we'd have children. Maybe we'd travel the world. Maybe we'd chase our dreams together.

Maybe. But now we'd never know.

When Kim asked Dr. Williams what he thought caused the cancer, he said only two words:

"Damn immunosuppressants."

Speaking of what-could-have-beens, Kailen's sister Kristen was pregnant at the time. Kailen got to see the ultrasound of "Peanut" and even made time to knit him a baby blanket. It was a special experience shared between sisters, but even though Kailen and I had accepted our childless fate long ago, it still hurt.

It also hurt that I knew Kailen would never live long enough to see her nephew come into the world. He would be born into a Kailen-less existence, and eventually, so would I.

Meanwhile, Kailen and I were still praying. We were still praying for a miracle and we were praying for God to give us a sign as to what to do regarding treatment. Neither option felt right. Kailen didn't want to do more chemo and she had vehemently refused radiation.

To be honest, we were both tired of fighting. It was like we needed someone to tell us, once and for all, that it was okay to let go.

And that's exactly what happened when we finally met with the radiation oncologist.

I remember it like it happened yesterday. He came into the room and sat down on the couch while I stood at the foot of Kailen's bed. He crossed his legs and rested his hands on his right knee. The sun was setting behind him, casting his face in shadow.

"I don't recommend doing radiation," he said. "At this stage, it would only extend life by a few months at best. The risks aren't justifiable."

I remember being heartbroken and relieved at the same time. When I glanced over at Kailen, I could tell she was feeling something similar.

"What about methotrexate?" I asked.

He shook his head. "You two have done enough. You've fought this harder than just about anyone I've ever seen. Your life expectancy is probably about the same with or without treatment at this point, so I recommend getting the heck out of here. Go do something fun, take a trip, lay on the beach. Enjoy the time you have left."

I remember saying thank you and shaking his hand, but there's a void in my memory after that, like something was redacted.

All I know is that eventually Kailen and I looked at one another, in the same knowing way we'd always been able to read each other's thoughts, and without a word the decision was made.

♥ ♥ ♥

It took us a week to get out of the hospital.

Kailen went through another series of lumbar punctures, where they repeated the dose of intrathecal methotrexate she had received back in July. The LPs were painful and traumatic, just like before, but they were trivial in comparison to the lung re-inflation procedure she had on September 4th.

Weeks of lying in bed with IV fluids flooding her

veins had led to yet another problem with her left lung. It was, according to the interventional radiologist, an "easy fix." But when Kailen came out of the OR, the expression on her face told a different story.

When I asked what happened, she simply shook her head as her eyes filled with tears. She didn't want to talk about it. And she never did.

The biggest challenge with getting Kailen home, or especially taking her somewhere on a trip, was pain control. Without the aid of chemotherapy, the narcotics were left to fight the losing battle alone. Kailen's pain was growing exponentially almost every day, so much so that even IV hydromorphone was struggling to keep pace. The thought of trying to manage the pain with oral therapy was laughable. But Dr. Williams and I, along with Kim and Jeff, had made it our mission to not let Kailen die in this hospital, at least not without making our best attempt to get her out.

So, Dr. Williams called in a pain specialist. The specialist analyzed Kailen's dosages and studied her usage of breakthrough therapy (i.e. the little red button you can push if your pain suddenly gets worse).

Using that data, he constructed a new regimen he thought would better manage the pain, and with the help of a local home health agency, got us set up with an IV pump we could take home. A nurse taught us how to use it, we signed all the necessary paperwork, and the next day, September 5th, after five weeks in the hospital, we finally went home.

Our plan was to rest for a few weeks at the house,

then hit the road. Probably head back to Hilton Head, then maybe swing down through Savannah and Charleston. The Carolinas were always one of Kailen's favorite places; the timeless southern flare, the warm breezes tinged with notes of salt and pine, and of course the dull gray, withering sheaths of Spanish moss – it all appealed to her sense of wonder.

After that, she wanted to see Fenway Park in Boston, eat a hot dog and sing "Sweet Caroline" with Red Sox Nation. After that, we would either come back home or keep going. It really didn't matter which, as long as we were together.

I was blessed to get a three month leave of absence from work – the result of some immensely generous pharmacists donating their vacation days to some kid they barely knew. It was the first time since meeting Kailen that my days weren't utterly dominated by all things pharmacy. I had studied and worked through some of the most difficult circumstances imaginable, going days and even weeks without sleep, leaving my ailing wife alone in hospitals and hotel rooms, slowly surrendering my humanity in the process.

But as I mentioned previously, I know my decision to finish school and start working was the right one. It had taken a lot of precious moments and racked my soul with guilt, but in return had yielded a priceless profit: A reason to keep fighting.

Only now, the fight was all but over. The white flag had been raised. It felt so wrong, like giving up, or worse, like a betrayal of divine trust. But once again, I knew it was the right choice.

Walking into our house was a feeling of indescribable triumph. Kim and Jeff stayed for a while and helped get things set up, then prayed over us and left us to the momentous task of re-establishing normality in the face of impending death.

Lucky for us (or unlucky for us), we had gotten pretty good at it.

When Kailen's bone pain worsened back in July, I had bought a smart TV for our bedroom. We didn't have cable at the time, but the smart TV allowed her to watch Netflix in bed, which was the only place she was able to get comfortable. Within minutes of walking in the door, she was posted up watching *Friends*. I brought her a snack, checked and double-checked the IV pump, which was propped in the bed beside her, and kissed her before heading into the living room to watch football on the digital antenna.

I didn't really care about the game; I don't even remember who was playing. All I know is it felt good to sit on a real couch in the quiet solitude of my own home.

A few hours passed, the game went off, a movie came on, and I kept checking on Kailen. She seemed to be doing reasonably well. She was resting peacefully, which I took as a good sign, and on about my fourth or fifth visit I accidentally woke her while fiddling with the pump. She was clearly irritated, judging by the vengeful scowl she gave me, but she didn't say anything.

Not a single word.

I should have noticed something was off, that her eyes were slowly glazing over. I should have done something.

But I didn't.

I kissed her forehead again and asked if she wanted me to quit pestering her. She nodded vehemently and I laughed. I checked the pump again. She was getting a basal, or continuous, infusion of medication, but also had one of those nifty little breakthrough buttons like she had in the hospital. The lockout period was currently set for six minutes, meaning the pump would issue a maximum of ten breakthrough bolus doses per hour.

Everything looked good and the machine seemed to be working properly, so I went back to the living room. I sat on the couch, watched TV, worked on my novel for a while, and suddenly it was almost midnight. When I got back to the bedroom, Kailen was just as I left her, sleeping deeply, her chest rising and falling in steady rhythm. She didn't stir much when I prayed and climbed into bed, but I wasn't about to wake her up again.

Friends was still playing on the TV, and though I muted it, I decided to leave it on. The light would allow me to see the IV pump better. It was still humming quietly, delivering her basal rate. She seemed so sedate I had the thought that maybe the dose was too high. It worried me, but she was breathing fine. Her rate and rhythm were both normal.

She's okay, I told myself. She's just exhausted.

Then I did the one thing I'll regret the rest of my life: I fell asleep.

When I woke up the next morning, she *wasn't* okay.

She was still asleep, her mouth slightly open, her chest still rising and falling, but everything was different. This wasn't normal sleep, I realized. There was something odd about the look on her face, the contortion of her body on the mattress. It was peculiar and unsettling, but I had seen it before.

Three weeks ago.

Kailen *wasn't* sleeping; she had fallen back into the pseudo-coma.

We would not be smelling the warm southern breeze. We would not sing "Sweet Caroline" at Fenway Park. We would dream no more.

By the time Kim, Jeff, and Jarrod got to our house, Kailen was dead weight. Her somatic nervous system had been so harshly bombarded that it had ceased to function. We first attempted to roll her out of the house in a wheelchair, but her agonized screams told us it was too much.

Her body trembled, her teeth chattered, her cries came out in gasps.

Jarrod and I picked up the wheelchair as gently as we could and carried her out of the house. The transfer into the car was torturous, as was the drive to Louisville, and despite a huge bolus of hydromorphone when we got to the hospital, Kailen didn't resurface. She drifted away from us, lost in that ethereal third space of consciousness, neither dead nor alive.

Dr. Williams told us he wasn't sure what had caused the collapse. It was most likely a combination of the pain and the cancer insidiously coiling itself around her brain. The symptoms were unpredictable, he told us. There was nothing we could have done.

I trust Dr. Patrick Williams as much or more than any person I've ever known. But I didn't believe him this time. He was lying.

Because it was my fault, I knew. Six minutes. Six. Minutes. The words echoed incessantly in my mind, like a horrible poem I couldn't forget.

Six minutes. If I had just pushed the button every six minutes, this wouldn't have happened. We'd still be at home. If I hadn't been selfish, if I hadn't been weak, she could have seen the ocean again. She could have died with dignity.

I just didn't know. I thought the dose was too high, not too low.

I didn't know. I didn't know.

I didn't know.

I don't think anyone expected Kailen to come back this time. The first coma had lasted nearly two days and she had only woken up thanks to the miraculous, and unexpectedly sudden, effects of the chemotherapy.

But now there would be no chemo. As tempting as it was to give it another try, it would have been foolish and selfish. All I would have had to do was sign the consent forms and the IV would have been running in less than an hour.

But I refused. It wasn't right.

Instead, Dr. Williams raised the pain medication dosage to unprecedented levels. It was the highest dose either of us had ever seen. It was concerning, especially as I watched her oxygen saturation drop, but it was the lesser of two evils. If she was going to die soon, there was absolutely no reason for her to be in pain.

The coma lasted through the night and all day the next day. Using her heartrate and oxygen saturation as a guide, we continued adjusting the pain medication as needed. Kim, Jeff, Jarrod, and Kristen were there, and extended family matriculated in and out throughout the day. If Kailen did wake up, no one wanted to miss it.

And she did. In the middle of the night.

I was busy wallowing in that sort of synthetic sleep common to hospital couch-beds when I rolled over and there she was, pushing her IV pole across the room.

"Kailen!" I shouted, drunk with exhaustion. "Where you going?"

She didn't even look back. "To the bathroom.

Even if you don't.

Obviously."

It felt like a miracle, and I suppose it was, but it was also further confirmation that pain had driven her back into the coma. The agony had been too much for a conscious mind to manage, so it had abandoned cogency and descended into hibernation. Only staggering doses of narcotics were able to lure it back into the light.

After the initial elation of another Lazarus moment wore off, the somber reality settled in for good. We were here for the long haul; barring divine intervention, we would never go home again. This room, number 583, along with the labyrinth of hallways and the rooftop terrace, was our manifest destiny. It would be our final adventure in this world, and then it would become our sarcophagus.

In the days following Lazarus Miracle II, Jeff, Jarrod, and I discovered an oasis. "Oasis" is probably a hyperbolic word choice, but that's what it felt like at the time.

We started taking tobacco walks (literal translation: *we walked and chewed tobacco*) outside the hospital. The landscaping was immaculate out front and there was even a peaceful garden area with a prayer pond. But that's not where our sojourn took us. Our spot was around back, near the doctor's entrance to the parking structure.

There, a small stream trickled alongside the building and wound its way beneath the interstate. It was far from picturesque – there was trash accumulated along the banks, the roar of traffic drowned out the gentle babbling of the water, and the whole place smelled sort of stale – but if you stood on that little foot bridge and watched the muddy water slip off to the southwest, you couldn't see the hospital. There was a thicket of trees, briars, and urban refuse blocking it from view.

It was a fragile fiction, of course.

That thicket had no power to erase reality. In fact, a few paces beyond it was the infusion center where Kailen had first received Remicade. And beyond that was room 583, where she lay dying.

The tobacco walks were a meager attempt at reprieve, but unbeknownst to us, they were actually serving a higher purpose. Kim later told me that our walks allotted her and Kristen priceless girl time with Kailen. It gave them opportunity to talk in the unfettered way women do when men aren't around. Even more, it allowed Kailen to say things she would never have said in front of me.

Put simply, it allowed her to be brutally honest.

I sat down with Kim a few weeks ago and she shared some of those intimate conversations with me. She shared Kailen in her most raw, unfiltered form:

"I'm ready to die, Mama. I just don't want to leave everyone. I don't want to leave my family and my friends. I don't want to leave Bryan. I don't want him to have to start all over. Do you have any idea how hard this is going to be for him?"

Even if you don't.

Or this comment, which K actually repeated to me later:

"I don't want our life to be like a Nicholas Sparks novel. We're just getting started. It can't be time for me to go yet."

But it was.

The seizures started the next night.

She was walking to the bathroom when suddenly her legs started to shake. Her knees would give out then she would catch herself at the last moment, which made it look like she was bouncing. I saw it all from the couch-bed and as she started to fall, I jumped up and ran to her, catching her right before she hit the floor.

Now her whole body was convulsing and her eyes had rolled back in her head. I lifted with all the strength I could muster, driven by adrenaline, and squeezed her thrashing body against my chest. I tried to lift her, to carry her back to bed, but I kept losing my grip. Her shirt was sliding up, her legs were kicking, and the IV lines were getting tangled. The IV pole itself was rolling alongside us, tipping and swaying.

"Okay, okay, okay, okay, okay, okay, okay, okay," she was saying, her cancer-invaded brain trying desperately to understand why her legs wouldn't move. "Okay, okay, okay."

She was slipping out of my arms. The convulsions were getting worse and I was getting tired. If I dropped her, her fragile body would break on the ceramic floor.

If she hit her head, it might kill her. Not to mention the IV lines would be violently ripped from her port, spilling blood and torn flesh all over us both.

With a surge of something like anger, I heaved with all I had and got us into one of the hospital chairs on the other side of the room. I fell hard on my back, she fell on top of me, and the IV pole fell on top of both of us.

"Okay, okay, okay, okay, okay, okay, okay," she was saying.

I squeezed her against me, quieting her body. "It's okay, baby. You're okay," I whispered in her ear. "Everything's alright now. *Breathe.* Just *breathe.*" I held my face against hers, hoping it would comfort her.

Eventually, the convulsions stopped and she came back to me. Her eyes saw me again and she calmed. But she was confused. And scared.

"Stay right here," I told her, propping her in the chair.

I hurried over to the bed and pushed the call button. Moments later, a nurse came in and helped us the rest of the way to the bathroom. Kailen's legs tried to give out several more times and more than once she seemed to forget where she was, but with a valiant assist from the nurse, I got her safely back to bed.

The next morning, while Kailen was still sleeping, I told Dr. Williams about what had happened. He seemed concerned but not surprised. The cancer was wreaking havoc in the neural circuitry of Kailen's brain; seizures were a logical byproduct.

But the concern came from the fact that seizures indicated progression, *fast* progression. He didn't say the words, but I knew the timeline was getting shorter and shorter. And after the events of the night, I found myself praying God would take her soon.

Watching her suffer was worse than living without her, right? *Surely.*

Three days later, September 13th, family came to visit again. It was a big group, Kailen's family and mine. They were gathered in the atrium near the terrace and someone had brought what seemed like a buffet of food, which was arranged across a number of end tables by the window.

I was talking to Kailen's grandparents and trying to eat something when I heard the intercom crackle above me.

Code blue. Room 583. Code blue. Room 583.

I looked around for a moment, then I started to run.

I was almost to our room, moving in a dead sprint, when I saw Jarrod walking toward me.

The color had drained from his face and his skin looked gray. "They need you," he said.

His baritone voice was calm, his posture relaxed, but

his eyes betrayed him. The pupils were dark pools of panic.

"What happened?" I asked, still running.

"Mom was helping Kailen to the bathroom and suddenly she was just gone. She couldn't hear us and she couldn't talk. It was...*awful*."

As we rounded the corner, I saw that our door was open. The room was full of nurses and I could hear Kim screaming. My brain was thinking too many things to really be thinking anything at all, but as I came into the room and saw the horrific scene playing out in front of me, I focused my mind on a single word: *equanimity.*

In that moment, my ability to contain my emotions and keep a level head was quite literally a matter of life and death.

Kailen was wearing green shorts with little pink watermelons on them (aka her watermelon shorts) and a light blue Mayo Clinic t-shirt. She either had on monkey socks or gray house slippers; I don't exactly recall which, but it had to be one of the two considering she never let her bare feet touch a hospital floor. She was sitting on the bedside commode, her head inclined toward the ceiling, while half a dozen nurses in blue scrubs swarmed around her.

"Oh, Bryan," said Kim, when she saw me come in. She had been crying and her body was trembling beneath the weight of the trauma. Her hands, ghostly white, were clasped tightly in front of her chest, as though she were trying to restrain them.

I stopped running and forced myself to walk, almost casually, to where Kailen was sitting. Kim frantically explained that Kailen had been using the bedside commode when suddenly her eyes started to roll back in her head. One moment they had been having a normal conversation; the next, Kailen was completely unresponsive.

It was an image no husband or mother should ever have to see. Her body was limp and leaning against the back of the commode, but just like the night of the seizure, as her autonomic reflexes tried to keep her upright, she seemed to bounce. Her head had fallen directly backward on her neck and she was staring at the ceiling, wide-eyed but unseeing.

"She's been like this for about two minutes," said one of the nurses.

"I didn't know what to do!" cried Kim.

Then a nurse was saying something else but I was no longer listening. I had to focus.

I felt a familiar cold rise in my chest and knew it was panic, so I swallowed it and steadied my breathing. There was noise and movement all around me, a clamor of concerned voices and shuffling feet, but I set my eyes on Kailen and refused to look away.

I put my hands on her cheeks and pressed my face within centimeters of hers, stared intently into her empty blue eyes.

"I'm right here, sweetheart," I told her. "Come back

to me. I'm right here. Come back to me, K."

Without changing the volume or the tone of my voice, I just kept saying it, as calmly as I possibly could. *"Come back to me, baby. Come back to me."*

It was the same thing I'd whispered to her during each of the Lazarus Miracles. But this time, she was even further away. I envisioned her walking through that idyllic field of wheat, moving toward the veil and the brightness beyond it, mere steps from her eternal relief. I imagined her running and laughing, her long hair blowing in some warm celestial breeze, no longer restrained by the shackles of her earthly infirmities.

I'm not so arrogant as to claim my voice was the only reason she came back, but I do think she heard it. I stood over her like that for a long time, what seemed forever, the tips of our noses nearly touching.

Her eyes remained vacant for several minutes. She wasn't convulsing like she had done during the seizure, but rather it was as if her body had simply been left behind. Her soul was moving on; her spirit was ready to leave.

But then there was me and my selfish begging:

I'm right here, sweetie. Come back to me. Please.

And she did. Again.

For the third time, she gave up Heaven for me, walked right up to the pearly gates and turned back around. Her empty blue irises suddenly grew bright as life flooded back into them. Kailen, my Kailen, rose to the surface slowly, but when she crested the water and came back into consciousness, it was almost as if she never left. She almost immediately smiled and cracked some joke that made all the nurses laugh and Kim cry.

I wasn't laughing or crying. I was too busy trying to get air into my lungs. I had ignored my adrenaline in a noble effort to stay calm, but now it rushed through my veins with such fury I thought my heart might explode.

I clenched my jaw and studied the floor. I was going to maintain my equanimity, heart attack be damned. But if I'm being honest, I wasn't thinking about equanimity. I was overjoyed that my beloved had come back to me, but unlike everyone else in the room, I was also overwhelmingly forlorn.

Because I knew three times was enough.

Actually, it was more than enough.

As Kim and I helped Kailen back into bed, I knew I would never ask her to defer Heaven ever again. The next time God called her home, I was going to let her go in peace.

Color is a beautiful thing.

That was the title of a Nina Simone song from the early-eighties. I'd never heard it or heard of it until one day in early September, when Kailen suddenly started singing it.

None of us, including Kailen, understood why, but the song was irrevocably stuck in her head. She sang it off and on for days until finally Kim figured it out – the song had been used on a paint commercial.

At some point, probably during one of our long, painful nights in the hospital, Kailen had seen the commercial and heard the song. Her mind, which was drowning in narcotics and being mutilated by cancer, latched onto the melody and refused to let go.

The day after the third and final Lazarus Miracle, September 14th, she sang it incessantly. If she wasn't singing it out loud, she was humming it, and if she wasn't humming it, she was asking someone else to sing it.

Eventually, Kim pulled the song up on YouTube and we sang it as a family:

Color is a beautiful thing
I know, I know
Color is a beautiful thing
I know, oh yes, I know
Color is the E Ching Ching
For sure, ding-dang
Color is a beautiful thing, I know

Despite being quite critical (apparently Jeff and I were flat on the "I know, I know" segment), singing the song together made Kailen very happy. Science would say her tormented brain was merely fixating on the song as a means of coping. But those of us that were there know better.

It wasn't subconscious fixation and it wasn't a coping mechanism; it was her way of sharing what she was seeing.

September 14th is what you might call The Last Good Day. Kailen was cogent all day, her pain was sufficiently managed, the nursing staff let us bring Rupp into the hospital and he curled up next to her, there were no seizures, and Kim, Jeff, Jarrod, and Kristen were there with us. I didn't know it then, but in hindsight I realize Kailen was already getting glimpses of eternity. She was seeing colors we couldn't even imagine. She was excited about Heaven and she was ready to go, but she was still human.

"I don't want to leave everybody," she told Kim. "There's so much more I want to do."

The thought of her not wanting to die raised my heartbreak to an almost untenable level. In the moments of agony when she had begged for death, I was able to romanticize the thought of her dying. It was a relief, a mercy, a fitting end to a tragic fairytale.

But when she looked at me and whispered, "Don't let me go to sleep," for fear that she might not ever wake up, I knew my heart would never recover from what was coming.

The Last Good Day was a Monday. Everyone stayed late; Kim, Jeff, and Kristen didn't leave until well after midnight. Jarrod stayed with us all night and pushed Kailen's breakthrough button while I got some sleep. I had slid the couch over next to her bed and for a little while, as we drifted off, we held hands.

Bryan C. Taylor

September 15th is what you might call The Last Bad Day, or more simply, The Last Day.

She woke up and had coffee – her favorite part of any day – but then her descent was swift. By lunchtime she had fallen back into the pseudo-coma. Dr. Williams increased her pain medication and we made sure to push the button the very instant it became available, our logic being that pain had driven her into the coma last time and pain medication had brought her out. Maybe it could happen again.

Maybe Lazarus could rise for a fourth time.

Unfortunately, pain was no longer the problem. The cancer in Kailen's brain was taking a devastating toll. She could barely speak, and when she did, the words were slurred and the syllables were misplaced.

At around 3:00 in the afternoon she began thrashing. She kicked her legs and tossed her arms, contorting herself sideways in the bed. Kim and I fought and struggled to keep her on the mattress.

She resisted for a while, with surprising strength, but eventually let her body go limp. When she did, her eyes burst open and she said her last audible words on this earth: *"Go get it!"*

I don't know what she meant, but after that, everything became very still.

Dr. Williams came by around 4:00 and we asked him how long he thought it would be.

"Probably by the end of the week," he told us. It seemed like a reasonable answer. But thirty minutes later, Kailen started gasping.

Kim, Kristen, and Jarrod were already there, but Jeff wasn't. He was on his way. Jarrod called him and told him to hurry, *really* hurry. It was now a matter of minutes.

We gathered around the bed and Kim played worship music on her iPad. I was at the head of the bed, holding Kailen's hand, feeling her final breaths brush against my face; Kristen was to my right, Kim and Jarrod were in front of me, and when Jeff came sprinting breathlessly into the room around 4:50, he stood at the end and held Kailen's feet.

The gasping continued. Heavy, deep, labored breaths tinged with mucus. Her chest shuddered as the air fought its way in and limped back out. Her lips were losing their color.

Around that time, it occurred to me that I must kiss her. It felt somewhat inappropriate, like I was interfering with her and her family's final moments. But it was my last chance, my final opportunity to feel her warm lips against my own.

So, I did it. It was quick, no more than a hug-phase peck, but I felt it as much as I ever had. Our romance never faded, not even on her deathbed.

Our first kiss was at 12:04 AM on December 18th, 2009. Our last kiss was at 4:55 PM on September 15th, 2015.

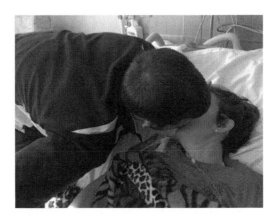

2,083 days. Our brief version of forever.

As Lauren Daigle's song, *I Am Yours,* played through the speakers on Kim's iPad, Kailen opened her eyes. Not wide, just slits, but they were open, and they were looking at me. Her head turned ever so slightly toward me, the implication obvious – *she was waiting.*

I squeezed her hand and whispered the words I had to say, the words I was born to say:

"Go to Him, sweetie. I'll be okay, I promise. You go to Jesus now. Run to Him. *You're free.*"

And then she was.

Kailen's spirit left her body before her breath.

She was still gasping intermittently, ten to fifteen seconds apart – the harsh, guttural, reflexive pleas of dying lungs. But there was a very specific moment when her spirit left the room, a tangible exodus when she, Kailen, was no longer with us.

It was in that moment that I finally gave up my quest for equanimity. I simply bowed my head and undammed my stale tears, watched with blurry eyes as they splattered onto her beautiful, lifeless arms.

I had never encountered such totalitarian emptiness. The room was cold and vacant, and I didn't need to look out the window to know the imperial nothingness had conquered the entire world. All that remained was the presence of absence.

As I stared down at her body, the reality I had accepted three years ago now seemed impossible. How could a human being, with all her quirks and nuances and loveliness, be so present in one moment and so completely gone in the next?

She had been my everywhere, and now she was nowhere. At least nowhere I could reach.

She was where she deserved to be, where I honest-to-God wanted her to be, but in all my time imagining what it would be like, the sleepless nights spent wondering how it would feel to finally lose her, to watch her die in my arms, I could have never created the depth of loss I felt when the actual moment came.

It was as if I had died with her, and indeed I had.

I heard Kim's voice first, then Jarrod's, then Kristen's, then finally Jeff's. They were singing. No one had moved from their spot along the bed, everyone was still crying, but they were harmonizing.

I couldn't get my vocal cords to vibrate hard enough to form actual words, so I just hummed weakly along with them:

Praise God, from whom all blessings flow;
Praise Him, all creatures here below;
Praise Him above, ye heavenly host;
Praise Father, Son, and Holy Ghost. Amen.

The Doxology. A proper goodbye.

Though my body was stricken with the paralysis of grief, someone went and got the nurse. She was young, about Kailen's age, and had become a close friend during our stay. She stopped in the doorway and placed a hand over her mouth as her eyes filled with tears.

She stood there a while, steadying her breath, until eventually she found her composure.

"I'm so sorry," she said. "I'll go page Dr. Williams. You guys take as much time as you need."

I won't share the details of the next ten minutes out of deference to the Combs family, but just know there were prayers, tears, and more singing. The notes were sorrowful, sung with grieving voices, but the words were worshipful, focused not on the loss but the gain. Together, we held hands and thanked God for giving our Kailen a peaceful ending to this life and a glorious beginning to the next.

By the time Dr. Williams arrived, I was alone in the room. Kim, Jeff, Jarrod, and Kristen had gone out to the hallway to inform the rest of the family.

The curtain was pulled so I didn't see him at first. I just heard the door open and the click-clack of his Italian loafers on the ceramic floor.

When he pulled the curtain back, he glanced at Kailen's body lying in the bed then looked over at me. I can only imagine what he saw. I was standing slumped in the corner, a man broken beyond recognition.

He held my eyes for a moment, his brow mildly furrowed, then walked over to the bed and felt for a pulse. He placed his fingers against the left side of her neck and pressed his palm against her chest. There was nothing; her heart was no longer beating.

He stood up straight, perched his hands on his hips, closed his eyes, and for an instant I saw his chest heave. But he swallowed hard and it passed as quickly as it came. He then leaned back down and kissed Kailen on the forehead, just as he had done on the day I met him.

As he walked over to me, I started to weep. He wrapped his arms around me, *firmly*, and held my head against his shoulder. I'm pretty sure he was crying too, but he didn't let me see it; he had conquered equanimity long ago.

"You did a good job, son," he whispered in my ear. "Stopping treatment was the right decision. You remember that."

"Thank you for being so good to us," I said.

He shook his head and looked away. "Thank you for sharing her with me."

To this day, I'm not sure if he was talking to me or to God.

I watched him leave and the nurse came back in shortly thereafter. She told me the folks from the funeral home were on their way and she needed to make preparations. I could leave or I could stay, it was entirely up to me.

I looked at Kailen's body. Being in the room was torture, but we had fought a war together, hand-in-hand. I wasn't about to leave her now.

As the nurse detached all the monitors and IV lines, I watched them hit the floor like chains being broken. Kailen was finally free, unshackled from the bindings of her earthly infirmities. The nurse and I gently removed Kailen's clothes and I looked upon her with admiration and agony.

The scars were everywhere – haunting vestiges of disease, infection, drains, and the countless surgeries that had utterly mutilated her body.

But none of it dimmed her beauty. Not even a little bit. She was as flawless to me, lying lifeless in that bed, as she had been walking down the aisle on our wedding day. To me, she had always been perfect. And now, in her heavenly body, she truly was.

With a damp cloth I cleaned her, washing away the stains of this wretched world one last time.

Then they came and rolled her away.

Even if you don't.

♥ ♥ ♥

Four days separated Kailen's death and her celebration of life ceremony, a timeframe in which there was little time for grief.

There was simply too much to do. Arrangements with the funeral home, selection and purchase of a cemetery plot, design of a gravestone, and then the actual planning of the ceremony.

The writing of the obituary was left to me. Seeing as I was her husband and an aspiring author, it sort of made sense. It would be beautiful, I told myself, the most eloquent obituary ever composed. The only problem was, when I sat down to actually write it, I realized my fresh grief had inflicted me with a devastating case of writer's block. It was more like a complete intellectual embargo – nothing was flowing.

I could barely think, much less write. After hours of scribbling and erasing, Kim and Jeff helped me get something down and we moved on.

It wasn't good enough.

But then again, how could it be?

The ceremony was held on September 19th in the sanctuary of New Life Church. Kailen's casket was set only a few paces from where I had proposed six years earlier. Friends and family made picture-boards and collages that were arranged along both sides of the altar. They were tastefully done, but I repeatedly tried and failed to look at them.

It felt adulterous. Pictures were a petty mistress, a promiscuous and grossly inadequate substitute for the real thing. They couldn't capture her in all her forms, her subtle poetic complexities. Their two-dimensions were an injustice that made me nauseous.

But I eventually looked at them anyway. Because even though I could still see her, embalmed there beside me, it was already beginning to feel like fiction. At least the petty mistresses convinced me it was real.

Unsurprisingly, the turnout for visitation was massive. For nearly eight hours, people flooded in by the hundreds and the line stretched out of the sanctuary, through the atrium, and into the parking lot. The ceremony crowd was no less impressive; there wasn't an empty seat to be found. It truly was a celebration of life, and this particular life was well worth celebrating.

We sang songs of worship and people lifted their hands all over the room. Pastor Tim Parish brought a beautiful and heart-wrenching message, and as he began his closing prayer, I looked around at all the people that had loved Kailen, all those her life had touched.

In some ways, it helped the pain. In others, it made it worse.

When it came time for me to speak, I shuffled onto the stage feeling more exhausted than ever before. I'd barely slept since she died and had eaten very little. As I stepped to the pulpit and felt the warm glow of the lights on my face, I was reminded of the first time I ever saw her, climbing the steps at Southland,

Even if you don't.

silhouetted by the neon glow of the stage.

There were so many things I wanted to say, so much I *needed* to say. But I knew the embargo wouldn't allow it.

I eventually croaked out a short speech, tear-soaked and piecemeal, but *out* nonetheless. I then read a poem I'd written about her. The audience likely thought I had written it for the funeral, but in fact I had written it on March 1st, 2013, two weeks before our first trip to Mayo.

I titled it, *The Vessel*:

> *There was once a man who fell into the sea*
> *The black waves tore at his body; the violent*
> *darkness ripped his flesh*
> *He shivered and struggled*
> *He tasted blood in his mouth, felt it in his eyes, in his*
> *soul*
> *He climbed to the surface only to be forced back*
> *beneath*
> *He fought, but time and again the swell claimed him,*
> *plunging him into the void*
> *As his body grew weak, the darkness grew stronger,*
> *fiercer, angrier*
> *He paddled and flailed but the sea was unyielding*
> *The blackness craved his life, hungered for his spirit,*
> *but above all it thirsted for his hope*
> *The man looked from horizon to horizon, from sea to*
> *sky, but death was all he found*
> *So he drew a breath and let his arms and legs fall*
> *limp at his side*
> *He began to sink*

Bryan C. Taylor

And then he saw it
There was a light, a small one, glowing like a
beacon in the eastern sky
It seemed so far away he feared he would drown
before it arrived
But he was wrong
In a blink the vessel swept past him, leaving him
bobbing in its wake
With all his remaining strength, he swam for the
ship, praying he would reach it in time
He did, and quicker than his broken body should
have been able
At first, he banged on the hull and screamed out,
begging the captain to take notice
But the ship didn't slow; if anything, it seemed to
gain speed
The man kept swimming, kept screaming, kept
pounding until his knuckles were bare
Then he saw it
Dangling from the starboard side, a rope skimmed
atop the waves
As he grabbed it with wounded hands, he looked up
the side of the ship
There he found the source of the light, the beacon
It wasn't an it, but rather a she
She was at the helm, but she wasn't holding the
wheel
Her hands were free, outstretched toward the sky
She possessed a rare beauty
The kind a heart can only know once
But as he stared, he began to see the maze of blood
and bruises on her arms
Saw the brokenness on her perfect face
She was like him, he realized
Hurt, tattered, stolen by the sea

Even if you don't.

But he was wrong; she wasn't like him
She was in bondage, but she wasn't a slave
She had fallen into darkness, but it hadn't consumed
her
She had the light
It shone so brightly that tears began falling from the
man's eyes
He looked ahead of them and saw only darkness
There was no certainty of shore or rescue
No lighthouse to guide them
But as he looked back up, he saw her shining, saw
her outstretched arms
He saw her hope
And with the whole earth dark around him, her light
was enough
It was enough to keep him holding the rope
And in that way, bruised and bleeding, the vessel
sped on into the unknown
Bathed in light

Kailen's Uncle Steve concluded the ceremony by singing *Fly to Jesus,* then the crowd began the slow trek over to Floydsburg Cemetery. The procession was more than a mile long.

Our immediate family gathered beneath a blue tent while hundreds of friends and extended family huddled in a semicircle around us. Kailen's Uncle Donnie gave a brief graveside message – something Kailen had requested in her final days – and once again, we sang The Doxology.

There were hugs and prayers and tearful goodbyes as people started filing out. Jeff, Kim, Kristen, Jarrod, and I were among the last to leave, and as we drove away I looked back at the cemetery workers slowly lowering the casket into the ground.

I would never see her again. Not in this life. But there was something that brought me peace in that moment, a sweet memory that held me together:

When I got as high as I could get, I inched along a thick sturdy branch. This was my favorite spot, because here I imagined I was anything. The sun shined the most here, so it looked like everything I wanted to be. It was my perfect place.

Kailen wrote those words when she was nine years old, in a story called *Maple*. I smiled as I looked back. Because rising high above the blue tent, casting shade over the interment, was a maple tree.

I stayed a week with Kim and Jeff after the funeral.

We spent time grieving together, reminiscing, sharing stories of the good times and tears of the bad. There were tobacco walks to the place we called The Field, cookouts at dusk over the fire pit, and of course, numerous trips to the cemetery.

I'll never forget the tears streaming from Jeff's eyes as we remembered the items we each put in Kailen's casket. I put my graduation tassels, Kim put a family heirloom Kailen had always hoped to inherit, and Jeff put the white stone we had given him from our honeymoon in Gatlinburg.

Even if you don't.

It wasn't until Jeff took out his Bible that we realized why he was crying. He composed himself and read from Revelation chapter two:

"To the one who is victorious, I will give some of the hidden manna. I will also give that person a white stone with a new name written on it, known only to the one who receives it."

Rock-hopping in that Gatlinburg stream may have made us late to our movie, but it provided the stone upon which Kailen's new name, her *Heavenly* name, was now inscribed. By all accounts, time well-spent.

On one of our last afternoons together, we took lawn chairs and sat in the shade of the maple tree, our feet dusty from the dirt of the freshly-dug grave.

"It's peaceful back here," Jeff said. "I think she would like it."

"She'd love it," Kim added. "Only problem is, I don't see a willow."

We all looked around. Sure enough, despite the large number of trees scattered throughout the cemetery and the woods that bordered the property, there wasn't a willow tree to be seen. Lots of maples, oaks, cedars, and pines, but no willows.

"Makes sense," I said, after a pause. *"This isn't home."*

We ended up sitting there together for hours, talking and praying, but as sunlight slowly faded and Kim and

Jeff made their way back to the car, I took a moment to stand alone by the gravestone.

I stared down at the image forever etched in the cold, black granite.

That fateful snapshot – me in my cap and gown, her in a purple dress, the iconic symbol of the victory we had achieved, the life we had lived – now stood stamped on her earthly resting place. It had once been a poignant reminder of all we endured, of our undying love for one another, and of God's faithfulness in the midst of tremendous tribulation.

But now, as a light breeze began to stir, it reminded me not of what-could-have-been, but of what-could-be.

It reminded me of all she had taught me. It reminded me that even though her death had seemingly taken the light from the world, there was still magic hiding in the dust. It reminded me that life can be a fairytale, even when it's a tragedy.

And most of all, it reminded me I was better off for believing.

Even though God didn't heal Kailen, and even though He offers me no assurance I'll ever rise out of the ashes of this grief and have the life I hope for, I'm going to take Kailen's advice:

I'm going to believe, and ask, and expect miracles.

Even if you don't.

Acknowledgements

Writing this book is among the greatest privileges of my life, right behind loving Kailen and being loved by God. I've dreamed of being a writer ever since I was a little boy, but I could have never imagined having such an important story to tell. Therefore, as always, the first person I must thank is **God**.

Next, I want to offer my sincere gratitude to you, **my readers**. My dream wouldn't be possible without your amazing support. But more importantly, you've helped Kailen's story reach the world. And for that, I could simply never thank you adequately.

To the Combs family – **Jeff, Kim, Kristen, Jarrod, and all extended family** – thank you for accepting me into your ranks. And as Dr. Williams told me on that final day in the hospital, thank you for sharing your sweet Kailen with me. This book, and so many of the stories in it, wouldn't be possible without you. I love each of you dearly, and always will.

To **Dr. Patrick Williams, Tracy, Ashlea, AJ**, and all the **amazing staff at Norton Suburban (aka Women's and Children's)**, thank you for loving us so well. Even in the direst moments, you imbued our fight with a sense of dignity. You provided quality care with a kind heart. I'm forever grateful.

To **Rembrandt** and the slew of surgeons and specialists we saw at **Mayo Clinic**, thank you for your excellence. You are truly world-class.

To **Team KCT**, I could never thank you enough for

295

your kindness and generosity. Your benevolence not only increased Kailen's quality and quantity of life, it made healing a tangible possibility. Though I can't list all your names here, please know it was a genuine honor to fight alongside you. Thank you for all you've done and continue to do.

To **Karena, Katrina, and the entire Tone It Up community**, thank you for giving Kailen yet another reason to keep fighting. You should have seen the look on her face when she won the Bikini Series. She loved her TIU sisters like family; thank you for loving her the same way.

To my mom, **Lesa Taylor**, thank you for planting this dream in my heart and diligently nurturing it through the years. And to my dad, **Steve Taylor**, and my sisters, **Audrey and Alyssa Taylor**, thank you for your willingness to read all the crazy stories I've written over the past two decades. Put simply, I wouldn't be me without you. I love you guys so much.

To **Alex Weires Scott**, the truest friend a person could ever have. Thank you for loving Kailen unlike anyone else, and for standing by me when few others would. I'm truly blessed to know you. Oh, and thank you for designing an amazing cover for this book! Kailen would be, *and is*, so proud.

To **E.E. Martin**, thank you for providing invaluable guidance along the writing and publication process. You helped make this book infinitely better, and I am thankful to call you my friend.

To all my test readers, especially **Brian Autry,**

Even if you don't.

Annette Merchant, Jordan and Megan Hall, Sam and Olivia McKown, Mat and Bethany Gillin, Chad Fromm, Ross Moffitt, James Humlong, Matt Scherrer, Ryan (Tom) Sawyer, my Kroger family, and dozens of others, thank you for investing in my dream and reading this book when it was raw and unfiltered. For a writer, there is no greater compliment.

Thank you also to my very **first reader and closest friend**. Your love and unyielding support, along with the faithfulness of Jesus Christ, saved my life. You know who you are.

Thank you to my **blog-readers and fellow grievers all over the world**. I pray the blog, and this book, have provided some measure of comfort amid the torrents of your bereavement. May the peace of Jesus Christ quiet the unending pangs of grief in your heart.

Lastly, I want to thank **Kailen**. Thank you for loving me, sweetheart, and for teaching me how to believe in miracles. And by the way, you're a published author.

About the Author

Bryan C. Taylor grew up on a farm in small-town western Kentucky, where his dreams of becoming an author had their origins on an ancient Dell desktop.

Not much has changed – Bryan moved to a larger town (albeit slightly), and now writes on an iMac as opposed to the old Dell, but the dream has always stayed the same.

Bryan has a Bachelor of Science in Biology and a Doctor of Pharmacy degree, both from the University of Kentucky. He was married for five years before his late wife, Kailen, the inspiration for this book, passed away from breast cancer at the age of 25.

Bryan now maintains a blog about grief and grief topics, where he seeks to teach others the lesson that Kailen taught him – *that life can be a fairytale, even when it's a tragedy.*

He lives in Frankfort, Kentucky with his dog, Rupp.

Find your fairytale (read the blog): www.bryanctaylor.com/blog

Connect with Bryan on social media:

Facebook: @bryanctaylorauthor
Twitter: @bctaylorauthor
Instagram: bctaylorauthor

Made in the USA
Lexington, KY
26 January 2018